# NIGHT LIFE

## Explorations in Dreaming

ROSALIND DYMOND CARTWRIGHT

A SPECTRUM BOOK

Prentice-Hall, Inc., *Englewood Cliffs, New Jersey 07632*

*Library of Congress Cataloging in Publication Data*

CARTWRIGHT, ROSALIND DYMOND.
   Night life.

   Bibliography: p.
   Includes index.
   1. Dreams. I. Title.
BF1078.C324 1977     154.6'3     76-30682
ISBN 0-13-622324-9
ISBN 0-13-622316-8 pbk.

© 1977 by Prentice-Hall, Inc.
*Englewood Cliffs, New Jersey 07632*

**A SPECTRUM BOOK**

10  9  8  7  6  5  4  3  2  1

Printed in the United States of America

PRENTICE-HALL INTERNATIONAL, INC., *London*
PRENTICE-HALL OF AUSTRALIA PTY. LIMITED, *Sydney*
PRENTICE-HALL OF CANADA, LTD., *Toronto*
PRENTICE-HALL OF INDIA PRIVATE LIMITED, *New Delhi*
PRENTICE-HALL OF JAPAN, INC., *Tokyo*
PRENTICE-HALL OF SOUTHEAST ASIA PTE. LTD., *Singapore*
WHITEHALL BOOKS LIMITED, *Wellington, New Zealand*

ROSALIND DYMOND CARTWRIGHT
is Professor of Psychology
at the University of Illinois,
Chicago Circle.

*To the pioneers
of the dark continent
of sleep:
the members of APSS*

# CONTENTS

# PREFACE

This is a book about dreaming as a psychological process. It focuses on the uses of dreaming and the relations of our daytime and nighttime mental lives. I have written it to present a point of view which has arisen out of my own work and that of my students over the past dozen years. I hope to share with the reader the questions I asked and the fun of the search for the answers study by study. This is the way knowledge grows, but after a while it is good to stop and ask: What is this growing to be, how does it all go together? What I have written draws on the work of others in the field, but it is still basically one person's view of the mind as it works round the clock from day, into night, into day. . . .

The roots of this book go back a long way. I caught my fascination with dreams early from my mother. She would recount her own dreams with such a sense of wonder at the ingenuity of the mind asleep, and took such delight in decoding the jokes they contained, that I learned to listen for the meanings with eagerness and respect. For this, thanks, Stella.

Much later when I wished to turn this avocational interest into a professional commitment to the field of sleep research, I was able to do so through the generosity of one of the first of this breed, Allan Rechtschaffen of the University of Chicago. He shared his expertise, his facilities, his time and help. He loaned equipment and supplies and gave me encouragement. He taught me the basic technology of how to recognize and record dreams in the laboratory. Thanks, Al.

Before this early enthusiasm and later acquired know-how could be translated into a research program, the help of many others was required. Melvin Sabshin, then head of the Department of Psychiatry at the University of Illinois College of Medicine, supported the development of the Sleep Laboratory there when this might have been considered an esoteric and expensive whim. Seed money to build and equip the laboratory was made available through his good offices from the university until grant support came from the National Science Foundation, the Department of Mental Health of the State of Illinois, and the National Institute of Mental Health. Thanks, Mel.

Once a laboratory and funds became available, it took assistants and colleagues to staff it. Here the list is long. Thanks to all of you: Ronald Hicks, Donald Williams, Jonathan Borus, William Pizzi, William Marx, Cornelius Palmer, Lawrence Monroe, Phyllis Walesby, Jay Sparber, David Williams, Alfred Kaszniak, Michael Haymes, Steven Gore, Martin Weiler, Sarah Labelle, Frances Marowski, Robert Ratzell, Roberta Barker, Rosemary Tegano, Lynda Weiner, Judy Hancock, Lois McCarthy, Elizabeth Butters. Aside from those who kept the vigil with me through the nights, there are those who transcribed the dreams, served as judges, made ratings, scored the sleep records, ordered supplies, and generally kept the shop running: Luberta Shirley, Linda Smith, Linda Kamens, Marti Bazell, Stephen Lloyd, Martha Arnold.

A laboratory, a staff, and funds do not produce research on dreams. This also takes people willing to participate as subjects. To all of those who have endured the collodion in their hair and the interrupted nights to share their dreams, my deepest thanks.

All of these ingredients are necessary but not sufficient to make a book. This takes the faith and support of loved ones who are willing to go away and be quiet while mother is working. Thanks, Christine and Carolyn. It also takes help with the production: the photos were done by Edward Retel. But mostly it takes someone willing to type, retype, check the spelling, correct the punctuation, and keep telling the writer it's OK. Thanks to you Martha.

# One

# WHAT IS A DREAM?

## Clinical and Experimental Contributions to a Definition

### *The Nature of Dreams*

What is a dream? Ask a child and he may say: "something silly or scary that happens when you sleep." Ask an adult and the answer, too, will often include the notion that dreams are not of our own making but that they are foisted upon us as we lie helpless. A man may be a daring explorer of the unknown by day, yet wake in terror from his dreams.

One reason for our sense of alienation from our night lives, in contrast to our feeling of belonging to our daytime world, lies in our own confusion of the two. During sleep we do not usually recognize that our dreams are in fact fantasized events. While awake, not only do we perceive a clearer distinction between what is happening inside the mind and what is happening outside, but we have the power to test which is which and to direct our attention from one to the other at will. When we shift our gaze from what is "out there" and focus on our inner response to it, or something that it reminds us of, we are aware that we are engaging in a different kind of mental activity, one in which our experience is an internal creation. Not so during sleep. We accept the imaginary for real and become as happy at finding a money tree in the backyard, or as upset at meeting a lion in the living room, as if these events were real experiences. Often in a dream we believe we must take some action to avoid or to obtain something only to find that things seldom go as planned. Objects and people behave unpredictably, and we are powerless to direct the course of events to our own liking as we can do with the imagined events of a daydream. The outcome of our night dreams is usually quite beyond our control. This quality makes it hard for us to recognize them as being our own creations.

Part of the definition of dreams, then, must be that, like hallucinations, they involve private perceptions which cannot be validated or shared by others, but which we accept at the time as reality, despite the fact that they may involve images and actions quite impossible in reality. We may talk to people we know to be dead, visit places we know not to exist, fly without any mechanical help, and while transcending all these laws of time and space, of cause and effect, only occasionally do we note, in passing, our own cleverness in so doing.

These "unreal" perceptions are most often visual, but they may involve any of the senses. The dream characters usually talk aloud, theme music may play, doors bang, phones ring. Textures can be felt, heat, cold, muscle sensations, and even odors can be recognized and take part in the story. While the body is at rest, asleep, the sensory system seems to remain active, creating a series of bizarre experiences which combine to make up storylike fantasies. The dreamer usually responds to these, not with direct action, for the body remains at rest, but with hallucinated action and with his whole emotional being.

When we wake, we quickly regain the distinction between the real and the unreal, and the memory of everything that so involved us just moments ago fades rapidly. No wonder that dream events, if recalled at all, seem amusing or puzzlingly alien to us. This difficulty that most of us have in being able to hold onto our dreams, or to bring them back at will, adds to our sense of their separateness from us. They appear not to be under our control at any point, neither in their creation nor in their retrieval.

Although the above features *describe* dreams as we experience them, we have left the question "What is a dream?" largely unanswered. Where do these images come from? What principles determine how they are chosen and organized into sequences? What is their relationship to our waking thoughts? Why do they arise at all? What is their purpose, if any? Why are they so difficult to recall?

### Explanations of Dream Origins

Many different explanations of the origins and purposes of dreams have been offered over the years. In some early civilizations dreams were thought to originate, not from within the mind of the dreamer, but from an outside agency, often a supernatural power, which put them into our minds to warn us of things to come. Pharaoh's dream in the Bible is one example of this. Holding the same view, the ancient Egyptians, Greeks, and Romans even built special temples where oracles gifted in understanding dream meanings could be consulted (Van de Castle, 1973).

A modern counterpart to this theory is represented in the work on dream telepathy—that is, studies testing the possibility that while we are dreaming our minds are more open to thought messages from others than they are ordinarily (Krippner, Ullman, & Vaughn, 1973). Perhaps dreaming is a state in which we can be influenced by others without our awareness, rather like hypnosis. There are certainly many popular legends of dreams which involve forewarnings, like Lincoln's dream of his own death just before his assassination. In almost every family there is at least one anecdote of a dream that predicted a death or some other unusual occurrence, of a dream that seemed to have the purpose of preparing the dreamer for this coming event. However, it remains a question whether these experiences were sent to the dreamer by some more knowledgeable person (divine or otherwise), or whether they were just visualizations of possibilities buried in the far recesses of our minds—kernels of ideas that may not yet have been formulated into conscious, waking thoughts, but somehow presented themselves during sleep as "ideas whose time had come."

Procedures have been worked out to test whether dreams can be influenced by thought messages deliberately sent by another person. Such experiments use two strangers who never meet: a "receiver," who sleeps in the laboratory and has his sleep monitored throughout the night, and a "sender," who stays awake throughout the night. When the receiver is asleep, the sender is given an envelope containing a group of pictures from which he randomly selects one to be the message for the night. A third person, the experimenter, watches an instrument recording the receiver's brain waves for signs that he is about to dream; at that point he signals the sender to concentrate on the picture. At the conclusion of each dream, the experimenter wakens the receiver and asks him for a report of his dream. In the morning, another person who knows neither the sender nor the receiver tries to determine which picture was involved in the test by reading these dream reports.

When we tried this method in our laboratory at the University of Illinois, only one out of six receivers clearly incorporated part of a sender's picture into his dreams. Strangely, though, the picture he "received" was not the one sent to him, but one intended for another receiver in the next bedroom. The picture was of a farmyard, with two small children playing on a haystack and a young lamb in the foreground. The receiver, a Vietnam War veteran, relived some of his worst war experiences in his dreams the night of the experiment. While reporting each of these, he mentioned with some puzzlement that a lamb was also present. Next morning, looking through all the pictures that had been prepared for the night's experiment, he had no trouble recognizing the lamb of his dreams.

Although there is little hard evidence of such outside influence on dreams, experiences like these make it possible to wonder whether the mind is in fact receptive to some kinds of telepathic stimulation during dreaming and that these may have some influence on the dream content.

The other common view of dreams, that they arise not from outside but strictly from within the individual, also has a long history. Plato suggested that dreams are outlets for the remnants of our historically primitive selves that allow us to tolerate being restrained and civilized by day. In the ninth book of *The Republic* he stated: "In every one of us, even those who seem most respectable, there exist desires terrible in their lawlessness which repeat themselves in dreams" (Plato, 1945, p. 297). This sounds very close to the modern psychoanalytic view. Freud argued that the purpose of dreaming is to allow repressed instinctual impulses to obtain satisfaction in the form of hallucinated fulfillment of these wishes. In other words, dreams arise to gratify the devilish desires unacceptable to our waking mind. This means they must operate undercover, in darkness and in disguise. This makes understanding them of necessity hard, and their recall prohibited. This is why special places and persons—the couch and the analyst—are needed for the decoding process.

Not everyone who explains dreams as a response to internal events claims that dreams have inherent meaning worthy of being recalled and understood. For example, according to the somatic or "indigestion" theory, dreams are nothing more than the response to distress following eating a particular kind of food, and so hardly worth the time and bother it would take to try to understand them. Among the more serious theorists are those who apply the analogy of the computer to an understanding of how the brain produces dreams. In this approach, it is suggested that the dream serves as a memory filter to screen the experiences of the day. During our off-line sleep time, we review and reject the redundant or inappropriate information not to be stored permanently. Dreams are made up of odd bits and pieces of junk to be discarded. They are hard to recall because they are not inherently meaningful: they represent only fragments of our waking experience. Since these are not the important parts, they are not filed in memory for future reference (Evans & Newman, 1964).

In contrast to this viewpoint, Alfred Adler (1936) believed that dreams continue the main lines of previous waking thought. Although the form of the thought changes with sleep from primarily verbal to primarily picture language, whatever it was that concerned us when we fell asleep is carried forward in this way. Calvin Hall (1973) put this position most clearly by stating that "dreaming is a cognitive activity transformed into a form that can be perceived" (p. 362). Implicit in this way of thinking is the intriguing notion that if our dreams continue to work on our uncompleted business of the day, we should be somewhat further ahead when we wake up—or at least further than if we didn't dream at all during that time. According to the computer model and to Adler and Hall, the relation of night thoughts to the previous waking experience is continuous, either in sorting it out or pushing it forward.

It has also been suggested that dreams deal with material quite different from our waking thoughts, that there is a real difference not just in *how* we think, but in *what* the work of the night shift is in relation to daytime thought processes. Perhaps this division of labor comes about because during wakefulness the mind is too busy dealing directly with the outside world to have time to attend to our internal responses to it. Or perhaps it is only during the hours when we are not required to make active responses that can we give our mind over to these inner voices. Then again, perhaps it is not just lack of time or space in our waking attention that makes dream thoughts so different in character from daytime thoughts; perhaps there is a real difference in *function* of daytime and nighttime thought. According to theories of this kind, sleep thoughts come from some other area of the mind and follow different laws of relationship from those operating in waking thought. Freud, of course, was the foremost champion of this position (Freud, 1955). In his view dream thoughts come from the unconscious, which is beyond our reach during the day. Dreams arise from a "lower" level of the adult mind, a part that used to control us at an age when we behaved principally on the basis of what felt good to us, without the constraints of what is socially acceptable, or even possible.

The Freudian model of the mind, in which different kinds of thought are seen to operate at different levels of the mind, has been challenged recently by a "lateral" mode, in which different thought modes operate literally side by side. Evidence is accumulating to support the view that the two halves of the brain, the right and left hemispheres, control different behavioral functions. The left hemisphere is specialized for language, mathematics, and logical, sequential thinking, while the right hemisphere is specialized for nonlanguage functions such as imagery, spatial and musical behaviors, and more holistic (nonspecific) thinking. Since most of us are right-side-dominant, right-handed, right-footed, and right-eyed, the left hemisphere dominates during the day, when we must be active in the world. It has been suggested that the right hemisphere is more active during dreaming, when thought patterns are of the nonsequential, imagistic variety. Evidence in support of this includes cases of patients with injuries to this area of the brain who report that they no longer experience dreams (Sperry, 1968).

## The Clinical Approach

Two serious routes to systematic knowledge about dreams, the *clinical* and the *experimental*, have been pursued by twentieth-century theorists. The first of these received its impetus from the monumental contributions of Freud, who provided both a systematic theory of all mental functioning, including dreaming, and a set of keys for unlocking the meaning of dreams. Dreams, along with free associations, formed the basis for psychoanalysis, which Freud developed for treating psychoneurotic disorders. During analytic sessions he urged his patients to recall and report their dreams, for his own self-analysis had convinced him that these were important sources for understanding what the patient could not tell him directly about the difficulties underlying neurotic symptoms. Freud also provided a set of operating principles for understanding the strange language hiding the secret messages the patient himself does not comprehend. The purpose of a dream, Freud believed, is to allow "the disguised fulfillment of a suppressed or repressed wish" (1955, p. 160), which must not be gratified directly. This is accomplished during sleep when the wish reactivates memory images previously linked with its gratification; thus we obtain gratification that we accept as real through the medium of highly condensed, multiply determined symbols.

Since each dream symbol represents many things, dream interpretation is of necessity complex, particularly since the whole point of the dream is to disguise its own meaning. What is more, understanding the meaning and tracing the origin of the surface story are only the beginning. As Erik Erikson has put it:

> Dream work uses certain methods (condensation, displacement, symbolization) in order to derive a set of manifest dream images which, on analysis, prove to be significantly connected with a practically limitless number of latent thoughts and memories, reaching from the triggering event of the preceding day, through a chain of relevant memories, back into the remotest past and down into the reservoir of unconscious, forgotten or unclearly evaluated but lastingly significant, impressions. (Erikson, 1954, p. 139)

The clinical position just outlined leaves the general public intrigued, but impotent. Dreams, we are told, are important keys to our inner selves, but they can only be understood by the expert—the psychoanalyst. Adding to the insult, this expert is apparently only available to the very sick or the very rich. The every-night dreams of the everyday person must remain mysterious, sometimes funny, often troubling, but quite inaccessible.

For the first half of this century dream interpretation was a large part of the treatment process as practiced by both psychoanalysts and therapists of other schools. The purpose of this pursuit was to carry out the central goal of the analytic process, which is to make the unconscious conscious by bringing unacceptable but still active impulses and fears into the light of day, and so bring them under the control of the waking rational mind. This method gradually became less popular as therapists came to feel that dream interpretation is too slow a route to health. Too often it became an end in itself, an interminable distraction, preventing patients and therapists alike from focusing on straight talk about reality. Nonetheless, Freud's theory of dream formation and its application to working with troubled people certainly helped make dreams an area of human behavior worthy of serious attention. Treating dreams as the "royal road to a knowledge of the unconscious activities of the mind" (Freud, 1955, p. 608) drew attention to the fact that there is more to behavior than meets the eye—and that there is material available, in dreams, which can yield knowledge to help us understand it.

Aside from pointing to dreams as an area of significance, the work of therapists who analyzed the dreams of their patients had another by-product. Gradually it became clear that our difficulty in recalling dreams, while a serious problem, is one that *can* be overcome. It was found that persons who claimed to have little or no dream recall could, within a short period of time, begin reporting one or more dreams at daily analytic sessions. This means that at least part of the problem involves neither a failure to dream nor a faulty memory. More likely, the problem is at least partly one of motivation and attention. As long as the culture considers dreams unimportant and people lack the resources for decoding them, there is very little incentive to pay attention to or remember them.

The increasing prestige and influence of Freudian psychology on popular culture through the 1930s led some research psychologists to seek to discover something about dream psychology in general. A few studies used home dream diaries, others the responses to questionnaires about recent dreams or repetitive dreams. These studies resulted in reports classifying the frequency of various kinds of dream characters, feelings, and topics. Dreams as a field of experimental research, however, remained a minor backwater to the mainstream of psychology, and anyone wishing to do serious work was up that creek with not much of a paddle. So far as formal psychology was concerned, dreams comprised an area of behavior too remote from direct observation or manipulation to generate data appropriate to the scientific method.

## The Experimental Approach

This Dark Age of dream investigation lasted until the mid-1950s. The Experimental Era began with the discovery of a set of reliable, directly observable neurophysiological correlates* of dreaming by Aserinsky and Kleitman (1953) and Dement and Kleitman (1957a, 1957b). Once experimenters zeroed in on the physical signs, in the sleeper, which indicate that a dream is in progress, they began developing laboratory methods for exploring the sleep state in an attempt to understand dreaming. With special equipment, we can now pinpoint when most dreaming is actually occurring. At last the dreamer can be brought into the laboratory so that some aspects of this behavior can be recorded directly.

From this work in laboratory-monitored sleep, we have been able to enlarge our definition of dreaming. The first new characteristic discovered about dreaming was that it is a highly regular event. Dreaming is not the sporadic occurrence it appears to be on the basis of our morning memories, but in fact occupies about a quarter of the nightly sleep time of healthy adults. Further, it has been found that this total amount of dream time is divided into four to six distinct episodes separated from one another by approximately ninety minutes of nondreaming sleep. This fact was established in a number of independent studies (Berger, 1969a), all using the indicators of dreaming first noted by Aserinsky, Kleitman, and Dement. These dream signs consist of a specific pattern of electrical brain wave activity recorded from the surface of the scalp, accompanied by a distinctive pattern of eye movement activity. Approximately ninety minutes after the onset of sleep, the recordings of experimental subjects wired to monitor this activity of the brain (using the electroencephalogram or EEG), and the movement of each eye (using the electrooculogram or EOG), show a dramatic change. The high-amplitude, regular, slow brain rhythm of deep, quiescent sleep ("delta sleep"), accompanied by slow, regular breathing, a slowed pulse and heart rate, and no movements of the eyes, gives way to an activated state of low-amplitude, fast, random brain waves, irregular breathing and pulse and heart rate, and large, very rapid

*Events occurring at the same time

conjugate (paired) movements of the eyes. When subjects are awakened during this pattern of activity and asked to report any ongoing mental activity, even those who previously claimed never to dream recall dreams, often in great and specific detail. On the average, 85 percent of all awakenings made from this sleep state, known as the *REM (rapid-eye-movement) state*, result in reports of dreaming, while awakenings made at other times of the night, in the absence of this pattern, yield very few dream reports (Berger, 1969a). The reports of mental activity which subjects give when awakened during other stages of sleep are characteristically different from dreams. When awakened from REM sleep, subjects typically report something like a short story made up of rather loosely connected perceptual episodes, often containing bizarre elements and characterized by a feeling of real participation in these events. When awakened during other stages of sleep, called *non-rapid-eye-movement, non-REM,* or *NREM sleep*, subjects report either that no mental activity at all was going on or that there were just "thoughts" rather than dreams. These thoughts are usually shorter, rather fragmented, and conceptual, and there is seldom any sense of active participation. Furthermore, subjects are usually aware of these *as* "thoughts" that are taking place in the mind (Foulkes, 1967). When awakened from a REM sleep, the report might begin: "Holy smokes! I was skiing down a mountain. Somehow I wasn't touching the ground at all, and I was dressed only in a pair of ladies pink panties. . . ." If the awakening had been from a NREM sleep period, the report would be quite different in character: "I was thinking about skiing, wondering if I could learn to do it at my age without looking ridiculous." The REM report describes a *dream*; it conveys concretely in pictorial action what is expressed in the NREM report as a thought under consideration.

This experimental technique—awakening subjects during different stages of sleep to sample the mental processes taking place at the time—lead to the discovery that mental activity is continous throughout sleep. Its form changes in cycles from being predominantly conceptual or thought-filled to being predominantly perceptual or visualizing, and back again. This gives a new cast to the thinking about dream instigation. Clearly, dreaming does not begin in response to some unusual somatic (bodily) state like a stomachache or to random external stimuli like a passing fire engine, although we cannot dismiss these influences altogether. Although they are not responsible for starting the dream process, they may influence the dream story.

Psychologists have written about several famous dreams showing the influence of external events on dream content. The most famous of these, quoted by Freud (1955, pp. 26–27), is probably that of André Maury, who dreamed in 1861 of being tried and guillotined during the French Revolution. He awoke to find the top of the bed had fallen and struck him across the back of the neck. An infamous dream, from my own family history, was told by a cousin, an inveterate card player. The dream occurred on a winter night. Her back was to an open window and a cold wind was blowing. The blanket slipped down, and her nightie up. She dreamed that she was playing cards. Someone looking over her shoulder at her hand questioned why she was not betting more on such a good hand. She replied that she couldn't because her "assets were frozen." This dream is a also a good example of the punning and assonance used in dreams.

The development of a technology for monitoring sleep processes in order to identify dreaming as it is happening made it possible to amass a good deal of factual material rather quickly. During the early years of this work, 1955–1965, researchers compiled figures showing how frequently dreaming occurs in persons of different ages, sexes, and intellectual levels. Next they explored the variations from these averages, particularly among persons who were ill or taking certain drugs. This work has made it now possible to make the following statements about dreaming:

1.  Dreaming is a kind of involuntary mental activity taking place during sleep with great regularity.

2.  It is characterized by perceptual experiences of a rather bizarre nature in the absence of reality testing (or recognition of their not being real).

3.  These experiences occur in cycles throughout the night at approximately ninety-minute intervals and extend in time anywhere from a few minutes (typical of the first dream of the night) to forty minutes or more at night's end (see Figure 1).

4.  The episodes are accompanied by a continuous, low-voltage, fast, random EEG pattern (Stage 1 sleep) and sporadic, rapid, darting movements of the eyes (REMs) (see Figure 2).

5.  REM sleep is present in the newborn in fairly high proportion (50 percent of all the infant's sleep is of this kind), and it is even higher in those born prematurely (Dreyfus-Brisac, 1964; Parmalee, 1968). The proportion of REM sleep to total sleep is reduced during the growing years. By the time young adulthood is reached, it occupies 24 percent of our total sleep, about half of the newborn rate. This percentage remains relatively stable until late middle age, when it again starts a slow decline, so that in old age there is somewhat less of this sleep proportionately than in the young adult (Roffwarg, Muzio, & Dement, 1966; Feinberg, Koresko, & Heller, 1967).

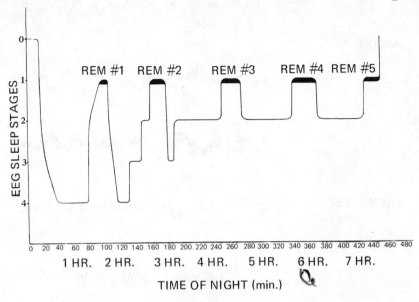

FIGURE 1. A typical distribution of sleep stages throughout the night

6. Persons of the same age group dream about the same amount. The range for normal adults is about 18 to 33 percent of total sleep time, and the number of rapid eye movements, which occur in the same person from night to night, remains remarkably stable (Clausen, Sersen, & Lidsky, 1974). Each of us tends to dream, night after night, at close to his or her own average amount, despite the vicissitudes of the day, unless we become ill or start taking certain kinds of medication. *Drugs!!! Downers!!!*

7. This fixed amount of dreaming can be experimentally reduced by awakening people each time their cycle shows they are about to begin the REM phase of sleep. When dreaming was first prevented this way, another characteristic of dreaming was suggested: dreaming apparently has qualities like those of human *needs* such as breathing or eating (Dement, 1960). Dement, who was the first to carry out the awakening procedure, noted that one effect of aborting REM sleep in this way is a shortening of the normal cycle length. When REM sleep is prevented, less than ninety minutes of sleep goes by before the sleeper attempts to shift from NREM sleep back into the active REM stage. If, as the night goes on, he is consistently interrupted so that no REM sleep time occurs, the sleeper will make increasingly more frequent attempts to initiate it. If this interruption procedure is continued for more than one night, less than an hour will be

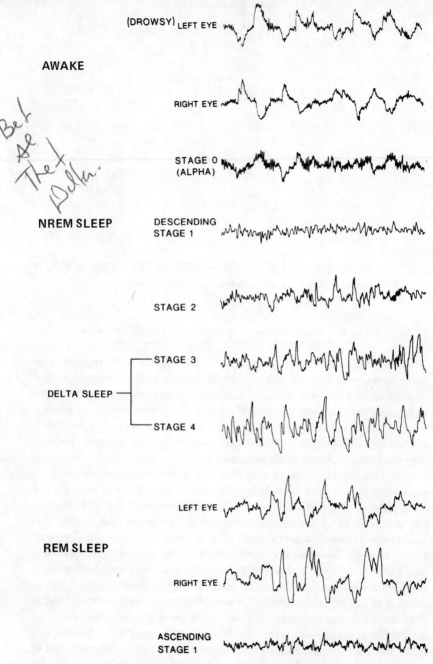

FIGURE 2. Electroencephalographic stages of sleep

spent in the first deep sleep of the night before the sleeper makes an attempt to have a dream period. The number of times a sleeper must be awakened to keep him out of REM sleep usually increases dramatically from night to night. When this procedure is stopped — much to the relief of both subject and experimenter — and the subject is allowed to sleep through the night again without interruption, he seems to go on a dream binge. These observations led Dement to suggest that dream sleep acts like our other biological needs: it builds up in tension until we are satisfied, and then tension reduces on a regular basis. When gratification is frustrated, tension increases even more until satisfaction is again possible, at which point the sleeper is likely to overdo it and "stuff" himself.

If dreaming is an activity which fulfills a need, the next logical question is: what need does it fulfill? This is the question that has kept many a sleep researcher up many a night.

In summary, based on their clinical experience with patients who report dreams, psychotherapists argued that dreams are an important source of information about an individual's subjective reality. Two different theories on the relation of waking to sleeping thought become prominent. One, represented by Freud and his contemporary, Jung, views dreams as complementary to conscious mental life, revealing the underlying unconscious half needed to better understand the total person. The other, represented by Adler, proposes that dreams are continous with waking thought except that the latter is carried forward in dreams in our more primitive language style.

Experimental work on dreams has resulted in a description of the distinctive psychological properties of dreaming and nondreaming thought. Researchers have also learned what kind of things we dream about. Most people do not dream of current events, political, economic, or world affairs, for example. Hall (1973), who was engaged in a dream collection project during the closing phase of the Second World War when the first atomic bomb was dropped, reports that none of his subjects' dreams showed any recognition or concern with this monumental event. What do dreams deal with instead? Hall answered: the realm of personal and emotional events and the dreamer's responses to them. On this point — regarding subject matter, what it is we dream about — the clinical and experimental approaches are pretty much in agreement. It is the question of their role or function which is much more controversial.

During waking hours, our attention is very largely directed outward, as we seek and respond to information from the environment. We can also redirect this focus inward at will to our present thoughts and feelings and to our memories of the past. Actually, while we are awake some processing of information from both outer and inner sources is usually going on simultaneously, though we don't lose the ability to recognize which is which. The important point is that we can freely select the material we want to attend to and shift the spotlight of our attention to highlight internal or external information. During dreaming, not only are we limited to inner stimuli—without being aware that this is the source of the material—but we have also lost the ability to choose from this pool the topic and how it is developed.

A central question concerns these two thought styles which we alternate between every day of our lives: Are voluntary waking thought and involuntary dreaming different ways of dealing with the same data, or is the stuff of dreams distinctively different from waking thought?

The best way to approach these questions is by first becoming acquainted with this material as it unfolds. This is the great advantage of the sleep laboratory. In the next chapter, we will explore what happens during a typical night in the sleep laboratory and what the sleeper and the experimenter can expect to learn there.

# Two

# A DESCRIPTION OF ONE NIGHT'S DREAM ACTIVITY

### The Dreams of Two Students Collected in the Laboratory

The discovery that dreaming is both regular and plentiful led to a good deal of curiosity about its nature and function. Using the laboratory method of monitoring brain waves throughout the night, we can capture almost all a person's dreams for study by awakening the sleeper as each REM period is ending. In this way dreams can be investigated more closely for their relation to waking thoughts and for the patterns of relationships among them.

The first question raised by the skeptic to all of this is: "What evidence is there that dreams have any inherent meaning at all worthy of our attention? Answers come from many authoritative voices, from the Talmud to Fritz Perls, all claiming that dreams are specially revealing. From the Talmud of the Jewish tradition comes the saying that "an uninterpreted dream is like an unopened letter." "But," our skeptic might reply, "this refers only to those dreams we recall spontaneously—without any technical help. We might recall these for a purpose, and then we need to 'read' them. Those we don't recall may be more like third-class junk mail, better discarded than opened. Not every thought that flits through our minds during waking is worthy of intensive study. Why should it be different for dreams? Is there any evidence that they are special in their content, or uniquely revealing?"

Many therapists believe that dreams deal with our most important personal emotional concerns, concerns that we may still know little about. On the premise that greater self-knowledge enables us to make wiser decisions and lead fuller and more satisfying lives, the increased access to dreams that the laboratory provides might supply valuable help in this effort.

"Perhaps," our skeptic might concede, "that may be true for the patient in psychotherapy who is struggling to understand his inner life and reconcile it with his behavior. For him the sleep laboratory might well be an aid to speed up the process; but is there any reason to believe that a person not in psychological difficulty can profit from this kind of more intimate knowledge of his dreams?"

The answer to this depends not only on there being some meaning worth discovering in dreams, but also on this meaning being easily discovered without the help of an analyst. Understanding a dream with the help of a psychotherapist is a very different experience than what ordinarily happens to the average subject in a sleep laboratory.

### Therapy versus the Lab: The Pros and Cons

One difference between these situations lies in the nature of the relationship between patient and therapist as opposed to that between subject and experimenter. Patients and therapists have a long-term commitment to each other, perhaps for years, with the understanding that, whatever comes up, the therapist will "see the patient through." Subjects and experimenters are rarely committed to each other for more than a few nights. The therapist has at hand a wealth of material about his patient's life to help him understand the meaning of particular dreams and interpret them to his patient. This is not just additional factual knowledge, but knowledge of a different kind. As the patient develops his sense of trust in the therapist neither to scold nor reject him, he opens himself progressively and shares more and more of his most private inner world. The experimental subject has no grounds for establishing such a level of intimacy, and he himself is usually lacking the required self-knowledge. Furthermore, the therapeutic patient's motivation to share himself is based on his desire to gain relief from some distress; the volunteer sleep subject's motivation for sharing his dreams is more likely to be a mild curiosity. The difference in the two situations is clearly reflected in who gets the fee: in treatment situations the therapist is paid for using his skill in helping the patient understand himself and increase his ability to bring his behavior under more rational control, while in the experimental situation the subject is usually paid for his time and trouble contributing data that the experimenter needs to understand some phenomenon.

Seen this way, the patient would seem to have the better possibility of arriving at some self-understanding through a consideration of his dreams. He has been trained to engage in the work of relating his dreams through associations to the rest of his life, associations that analysts believe are essential in unraveling a dream's many meanings. The experimental subject has not been prepared to work in this way and has no special motivation to do so. What is more, there is some evidence that the dreams collected under the public conditions of the lab are blander, not nearly as personally exciting as those which the same subjects experience in the privacy of their own homes (Domhoff, 1969). They certainly do not contain as much sexual or aggressive material. Yet there are some clear advantages to analyzing the dreams collected in the laboratory which make it possible for both psychologists and subjects to gain something of real value from looking closely at them. This is true even of those dreams that make up just one night of REM awakenings.

One advantage of the laboratory situation is that *all* the dreams of the night may be retrieved, not just the last one, which is typically the home situation. This means that not only are there four or five times as much dream data available after a night in the lab, but it comprises the whole story of the night's dream activity, not just a fragment of it. If during a night's dreams there is a continuing line of mental activity, having only the last dream to work with is like trying to understand a book by reading a chapter out of context, a difficult chore that requires great interpretative skill. In addition, of course, the dreams of normal subjects who are not suffering from acute psychological disturbance may well be easier to work with. Perhaps when there is less material which has been banned from awareness and less anxiety, dreams undergo less symbolic coding. In this case, the laboratory dreams may be more open and direct.

Another advantage to studying dreams in the laboratory is that dream reports are less subject to the distortions and changes that occur with time delays. Subjects awakened in the middle of the night have less opportunity to change dreams in ways that shift their emphasis or rationalize wishes than do patients who must wait for hours or days after the dream experience before retelling it. In light of all this, laboratory dreams may not be such a bad bet for yielding up obvious dream meanings, if they are there.

## Two Dreamers

The best way to answer the question of what might be learned from the dreams produced during a night of laboratory awakenings is to look at some examples. Jerry and Don* are two typical subjects whose dreams were recorded on the same night in our laboratory. They were both freshmen medical students in their early twenties. Neither was married, and both were very bright. They were in good physical and psychological health. Neither had any special interest or training for dream recall. Both said they ordinarily remembered only about one dream a week. However, on the winter's night that they were awakened from their sleep with electrodes in place, each produced five dream reports, one from each REM period. They had each slept in the laboratory for the two previous nights without being awakened in order to adapt themselves to the situation of being EEG-monitored. They were told that on the actual night of the experiment they would be awakened "several times" and asked to report any mental activity occurring at the time. We impressed upon them that they might find they had no recall at all, or that they had been thinking or dreaming or having some other experience. Any and all such reports were equally valuable to us. Most important was that our subjects be as accurate as possible in their reports. (See Figure 3.)

Since the first REM period of the night is typically very short, usually not more than five to ten minutes, the first awakening was made five minutes after the onset of the first signs of REM. All other awakenings were made ten minutes after each subsequent REM period began. Why not wait until the end of the REM period so that we might know the whole dream story? Because the ability to recall the dream fades very rapidly once this stage of sleep is over; waiting till the end risks losing it all. In the morning each subject was asked to review all of the dreams of the night that he could remember and to add any information that he may not have remembered to tell before.

### JERRY AND HIS DREAMS

Jerry was a tall, rangy, farmboy from downstate Illinois, a young Jimmy Stewart type, rather shy and unsophisticated. When he was awakened the first time he reported:

*Although all the dreams reported in this book are actual reports collected in the laboratory, the subjects' names are fictitious.

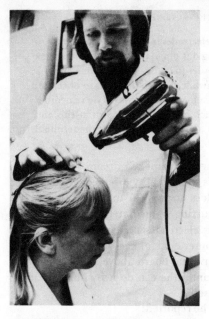

GETTING ELECTRODES ON

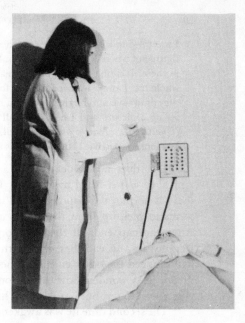

PLUGGING IN

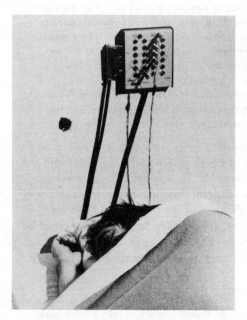

ASLEEP

AWAKENING FOR A REPORT

FIGURE 3. The sleep laboratory at
University of Illinois, Chicago Circle

I was playing with the leads from these electrodes in my mind, and trying to figure out where they went. I was pulling out plugs and putting others back in there. It didn't seem to be any real order to it. I can't really remember a whole lot. I know I played around for awhile. I stuck the leads in once and they didn't seem to be right, so I put them in a different way. I do remember seeing a picture and I had them all stuck in a little box down at this end (*Question: You saw a picture?*) Well, in a mental image, what the terminal box looked like that I stuck the leads into.

This does not appear to be a very "dreamlike" dream, but this is typical of a first REM awakening. It is quite reality-oriented, it is short, there is no plot development, and it does not appear to be emotional. It seems to pick up from the events occurring immediately prior to sleep. After the cap ends of the monitoring electrodes had been attached to Jerry's scalp, his earlobes, and at the outer edge of each eye, an assistant had plugged the other ends into the terminal board above his bed. In the dream Jerry wonders how this is done and if he can do it by himself, and goes ahead to try, but is not sure of himself.

The second time he was awakened he reported:

We were driving in a car coming down here and I remembered we stopped and I think it was Forty-first Street. We had to stop at a stop sign, and the stop sign was turned around the wrong way. We weren't sure if we had the stop or the other guy had the stop. I think we stopped and he just about stopped. Finally he kind of eased to a stop and then we went on. There wasn't any snow on the ground and there weren't many buildings either for some reason. Don was there, and, I guess, Mr. H. We had Mr. H's Volkswagen. Well, wait a minute, Mr. H. wasn't around on the trip . . . let's see . . . I remembered Don and I were going south on the Outer Drive. We were coming down to this place and we didn't really know how to get there, and there was a stop sign on the Outer Drive at that point.

This dream has a little more distortion, although it is still close to reality. Actually, that night Jerry had been driven to the lab along with the other subject, Don, by a lab assistant, Mr. H, who did drive a Volkswagen. The distortions in the dream from the real situation involve the absence of Mr. H, of snow, and of the buildings, and the presence of the stop sign. There is no sign, nor any cross street, at Forty-first Street, so there could be no confusion about the right-of-way. The theme again involves some confusion about the right way to do things and the absence of the authority person who knows how.

The third time he was awakened Jerry reported:

I dreamed I was going to the Chicago Public Library to take a book back and then I pulled up in front of the library and walked in and everything went normally, and then I had a terrible time finding the right place to take the book. I know I got rid of the book. The library looked quite a bit like the library down at the University of Illinois at Champaign. It seemed like the Chicago Public Library was sitting about where Cook County Hospital is now, 'cause I remember I met somebody in the library and they were going to go across the street to the Greek's [ restaurant]. I don't remember ever leaving. I didn't have the book anymore, but I was still in the library.

This is the first example of the development of a condensed symbol, the Chicago Public Library, which Jerry dreams is like the library of his undergraduate days and is in the location of the hospital in which he may well have classes and see patients in the future. It would seem to stand in general for his educational institution. Again the theme is one of not quite knowing how to handle some routine and feeling a little anxious about it. This is the third dream in which the subject is without an authority figure around to help, trying to manage on his own some confusing aspect of his new environment. These move in time from the immediate present and a specific lab event to his more general present life.

In his report from the fourth awakening Jerry makes a large jump back in time:

I was making mud pies. I remember sitting there on the ground which was fairly hard . . . kept having to add water and then I finally got the mud — there must have been a gallon of it — stirred up pretty well until it was just a little bit thinner than cake dough, looked like cake filling, and I was just getting ready to pat it out into little round patties when you woke me up. I had one person helping me, this was some girl, I don't seem to remember her at all. All she did, I think, she got the water because I know that I stirred up the mud, used a stick to do it with. The day was pretty, bright, and sunny, I think it was summer too because I didn't have anything much on. Let me see, I remember I was making the mud pies. I would guess them to be about eight inches across. They looked pretty round to me, too. I was using a paint-stirring stick. I remember the mud was brown. It was kind of brown mud, it was sandy too. I remember that. I remember stirring it up, it had grit in it.

Here there is a change not only in time but also in mood to a period when life was simple. This may be a wish-fulfillment dream: "Oh, to be a child again, sitting in the sun, with nothing more complicated to do or learn than making mud pies with a little girl helper."

At the last sleep interruption Jerry continued the back-home theme:

My mother was giving me a bath and that was about it. I was sitting in a high chair and when you woke me up I was getting my ear washed. I remember seeing the sink on the wall and Mom had water in it and she was rinsing out the washrag, it was a white washrag, and then she washed my face and then she had a hold of my earlobe and was pulling it out and cleaning the inside of my ear. I looked like I might have been about four. Mom was wearing light brown slacks and a white sleeveless blouse. I think I remember how it got started. I remember the last time [that you woke me] I was just getting ready to go to sleep that I put my hand on the back of my neck and I felt pimples back there and I figured maybe I ought to start washing a little bit more and then when I went to sleep I guess I started dreaming about having my face washed.

As Jerry continues his backward progression in time, he is being cared for by his mother. His own interpretation of the dream is that it was triggered by finding the pimples on his neck just after his last awakening and giving himself the good advice, as his mother might, to wash more often. This dream might also appear to lend itself to a wish-fulfillment analysis, since he has been saying in Dreams 1, 2, and 3 that it is hard to take care of everything in a new and complicated world, and then in Dream 4 that it might be nice if he were small again, and in Dream 5 that if he were small, his mother would take care of these things for him. This, however, is not the whole story, since the emotional tone is wrong. He is not enjoying being cared for. He is passive, but angry. The mother figure not only represents his own mother, it is also clearly myself. It was I who put him on a stool (high chair) to attach the electrodes for the night. During that process I scrubbed his earlobes with a white sponge soaked in acetone which I had explained to him was to clean the skin. Thus we have another example of condensation: the female-helper-mother-knowledgeable-authority are condensed into a single symbol of those who through "helping" take charge and put him down and make him angry.

In the morning when he was asked what he remembered, Jerry recalled all of the dreams except the first one. When he was reminded of it he replied that there was "not a whole lot to it, really, except I was playing around and I didn't know which lead went where. The receptacle looked a lot like the one at the head of the bed. I could see it pretty clearly." When I asked him how realistic an experience this was, he said:

I would say pretty close to reality. This is something about me, I guess, I feel a little bit, all these . . . a little bit silly at not being able to do something. If there is a skill or something that I can't do and I have reason to possess it, the first thing I always want to do is learn it. If there is something I have to do and I don't know how, it kinds of burns me up that I can't do it. The first thing I usually do is go about trying to learn, and in the process, if somebody comes along and says, "Hey, you don't know what you are doing, let me show you how," that isn't quite so bad, but if they come along and say, "You better go along, you don't know how to do this. Let somebody who knows what they are doing do it," oh, that usually burns me up. That's cause for war when they do that. I couldn't say for sure, I'm not much of a psychologist or psychiatrist, but I do remember that I was working *feverishly* to get the plugs in the right holes before you came along and stuck them where they should be yourself.

When he was asked whether the dreams were pleasant, unpleasant, or neutral, he labeled the first, second, and third as neutral, the fourth (the mud pie dream) as pleasant — "there is nothing like making mud pies" — and the last dream about having his face washed he called "unpleasant." "I always hated to have my face washed. Anything I *hated* was having my face washed." Following his report, being sensitive clinicians as well as experimenters, we invited him to unplug his own electrodes from the terminal board, which he was pleased to do.

There is much we could say about the meaning of this group of dreams as a whole. The theme for the night as stated and restated in the first three dreams appears to continue the feelings of anger engendered by the threat posed to his already-shaky sense of competence by the rather complicated laboratory reminding him of other instances of his ineptitude. His first solution to this problem in Dream 4 is to regress to the simpler life of childhood, but this is entertained only briefly before being rejected in the feeling of the last dream. Although the mud pie dream gives him the complementary feeling of competence and self-assurance, he reminds himself in the earwashing dream that this period, too, was accompanied by a sense of frustrated self-esteem because of his helplessness in the hands of authority figures.

Despite the fact that this was not a therapeutic situation and there was no attempt to help this student work with his dream material or delve into its deeper meanings, Jerry reached his own understanding of a major character problem underlying all of these dreams. Some weeks later, at the end of his participation in the experiment, he was asked what he made of his dreams and if he saw any way in which they were all related to each other. The following paraphrases his response:

They all followed from that first one about trying to figure things out for myself and not being sure I can do it right. This place really has me working to keep up. I'm just a country boy, and I've never lived in a big city before. Guess I've always been like that, though. My father always gave me impossible jobs to do, like keeping a second-hand car running for him. If I couldn't fix something, boy, he really blew up. He would never buy new parts but always had three or four old junkers around, and if I needed something, I had to rob the others to keep one going. It was impossible. I had to keep trying, but I could never win. I thought I left that frustration all behind me with the hicks and the turkey farmers, but I guess I haven't because I still get mad talking about it and I guess that's what made me dream about it.

His present general sense of incompetence was brought sharply into focus in the lab. This touched off similar memories from the past. Only one dream, the fourth, is complementary in theme and feeling to the others.

## DON AND HIS DREAMS

In contrast to Jerry, Don was from a big city. He was sensitive, intellectual, and humorous, a Woody Allen type. Would he, too, show an anxiety response to sleeping under such strange circumstances and relate this to his old anxieties, or would he be "cooler" about the whole thing? When awakened the first time, Don reported:

I'm in a boardinghouse arrangement like I live in now except everybody in there, including myself, don't particularly like one tenant and so during the night one of them kills him and says it is all our duties to help him. And so he gets some sort of paper to wrap him in. It's wet, like sticky, paper. It had a trade name, and we were in the midst of wetting it and applying it. Everybody in the boarding house was working together. It was an old house very much like the one I live in except the rooms were bigger and for some reason everyone could see into everyone else's room through a little grate in the floor or the wall. I don't know what it was there for, it was the reason that everyone didn't like this particular tenant. The person who killed him was a sharp organizer type, kind of short but compensating for it by being very pushy, very bossy person. He organized the whole boardinghouse immediately after disposing of the tenant. He is the only one that I can remember there. He unrolled the paper and then had his girlfriend or something [that] would go and get some sort of liquid. We'd all seem to get a share of it and we'd all apply it to the paper and the short guy was very careful, he said to her to save the receipt for the liquid [because] it could get us into trouble. It had the consistency of unhardened gelatin and we all applied it and rubbed it into this paper and he would take sections of it and leave saying he was using it to get rid of the body. The girlfriend was not very pretty at all, stocky, long black hair. It may have been another boarder who liked him and so was doing what he wanted.

This dream report is more developed than most from a first REM period, and it shows how much material can be experienced in the first five minutes of this stage of sleep. It also shows the combination into a new set of images of two presently anxiety-provoking reality situations. The first of these appears to be the sleep lab itself and not being sure whether to trust the pushy organizer (Mr. H, the lab assistant) and his black-haired girlfriend (myself). These two seem to be up to no good with their paper

(EEG paper) and gluey liquid (collodion) and their rooms through which you can be observed. In the lab, subjects actually come into the control room to have their monitoring electrodes applied. Getting the electrodes to stay in place during the night involves gluing them down with collodion, a very sticky substance. While this is happening the lab assistant is typically engaged in getting the EEG equipment ready, inserting a large package of paper (enough to last the whole night) into the machine, and testing the intercom system for collecting the dreams. Some of these images were clearly incorporated into Don's dream.

The second anxiety situation represented here is Don's introduction to his first cadaver in his gross anatomy lab, which he talked about while he was being prepared for his night of sleep recording. The body of an adult male had been presented for dissection, wrapped in brown paper. This shook him up a good deal. The two lab situations both involved anxiety about someone lying prone (himself and the cadaver), and both involved paper and glue. These were amalgamated in the dream. There is a question about why this dream was set in the boardinghouse, which he recognizes as his own. This raised the question in my mind: What is going on there that is also making him anxious about sleeping or death?

The second awakening produced this dream account:

My father used to have a drugstore right in the middle of the bad black neighborhood on the South Side. It was always touch and go with the population around there. We avoided them in order to avoid any difficulty, and where we are now is also a black neighborhood and the whole thing is being repeated again. In the dream I found myself and a friend of mine being followed by a couple of junkies, about forty to fifty years old as we were walking along. It looked like we were going to have a lot of trouble because they were getting belligerent and so I went into a store that I knew and started calling my father in his store which apparently wasn't too far away, and I get an operator on the telephone and for some reason she can't understand what I am saying. I'm saying Sixty-third and Cottage Drugs and she doesn't understand no matter how many times I say it. She doesn't understand what I am talking about and it's important that she does because we've got to get out of there, but she just won't understand. The friend was somebody I had gone through high school with, just one of my friends that was with me in undergraduate days but I haven't seen him since. He had never been on the South Side before and he wanted to see what it looked like. He had me show him around and he was very, very nervous about the whole thing. And when this incident occurred, he apparently saw that I was a bit nervous myself. The two blacks were very degenerate low-class types, who were a bit drunk and very nasty. They asked my friend for a dime and he gave it to them. Then they asked him for a dollar and he wouldn't give it to them and they started following us. I made the phone call from a drugstore that belonged to one of my father's competitors in the old store. I went in and asked for the man I knew but the store had changed hands and he wasn't there, but I knew where the phone booth was and I went back with my friend to make the call. I had genuine apprehension when we couldn't get in touch with my father and I knew we couldn't go outside or turn to the people in the drugstore, and that we were trapped in there so there was nothing we could do. I remember feeling fear there, and that's all.

Many of the elements of this dream seem to represent a continuation of the same anxiety about the laboratory present in the first dream. Both in the laboratory and in the dream Don finds himself trapped in closed quarters, menaced by strange, sinister people, and is afraid he will not be able to make himself clearly understood to a lady operator of a communication device. The feeling connected with the first dream seems to have reminded him of similar feelings of threat in the past when he lived in bad neighborhoods. His father, who might be of help, is out of touch, and Don's imagination is unable to create any closer source of support. There is a suggestion here that he and his buddy are in trouble because they won't go along with, or pay the price for protection from, the degenerates.

The third awakening produced a dream report very different from the first two:

I was sitting in an open-air cafe in Paris and looking around at all the people that were sitting there and one by one I'd stop and look at them and I could hear movies and a voice from the background was saying, "This is so and so, and such and such." I was supposed to go on from there but I never did. There was something like the "noble Duke of Something," very weird. No plot, just a nice frosty fairy tale. A very large open-air cafe with many, many tables, most of them filled. Everything expensive. Looking out over the street, and apparently sipping Bordeaux.

This dream represents an escape from the phone booth and the terror of being menaced by the drunken, lower-class men. It is in every way the opposite of the last dream. It is four thousand miles away, in an open rather than a confined space, one in which he can look at people face to face rather than fear them coming up from behind him. He lingers there by choice, sipping wine in luxurious surroundings among nobility rather than being trapped by degenerates. Clearly this is the wish-fulfillment solution to his anxieties about his ability to cope with the threat of physical, perhaps even homosexual, attack—an interpretation that is supported in later dreams. Like Jerry's mud pie dream, it represents an escape from the problem rather than a solution, and it doesn't really satisfy him for long. Even Don recognizes this while telling it and calls it a "nice frosty fairy tale."

On the fourth occasion he reports:

> Something to do with a horse. There was a very nice-looking girl and I was giving her riding lessons. I [first] found myself on a horse in a ground-level apartment and we left and went for a ride in the park district area. Then there were a couple of girls ahead and the kid I was riding with; I took one [girl] and he took the other, and they asked if they could ride and we said yes, and the girl that I was giving riding lessons to had black hair, and she was nice-looking, she wore leotards. [Before] when we were back in the apartment, the horse pushed his way into the kitchen, seemed to know what to hit to open the refrigerator where it was making ice cubes. It had two ice cubes in its mouth when it went into the streets riding and then to the park. When the girl got on the horse, she decided that it was best for making it . . . it was easiest to make it go faster by taking a fountain pen and jamming the point into the horse's rump and it worked.

This dream of teaching a nice-looking girl to ride horseback seems to be symbolic of a heterosexual relationship. The fact that it follows the escapist fairy tale supports the interpretation that his next defense against a homosexual temptation would be a heterosexual commitment. This is confirmed by the dream's beginning with him on a horse inside an apartment with a "kid," a male friend. The horse then gets cooled off with two ice cubes, and he and his friend proceed to pick up two girls in the park. His girl, although attractive, behaves according to a more masculine sex role by jamming the horse in the rump with something sharp (phallic) to make him go faster. As with all interpretations, this one must be tentative pending some support from another dream.

The last recall of the night continues this theme:

> We wanted to go see Barbra Streisand at the Stadium and we had two tickets. We arrived a little late and there were no parking spaces so we didn't go. We started back and we were going to see a movie. At the S-turn on the Outer Drive, we got into some sort of an accident and held up traffic there. This girl I had taken in her car — which is, as I remember, the reason that I took her to the concert was that she had a car — she is some girl in my class here in school. I don't like her very much at all. She is not very pretty and so she compensates by not being very nice also. One of the reasons I had the accident on the S-curve is that it was packed with 150-story buildings on both sides of the street. They had built these towering, towering skyscrapers and I had never seen these before and I was so shook by all these that I was looking at the skyscrapers and I went straight instead of turning and just hit a wall.

This seems to support the interpretation that Dream 4 is an attempted resolution to anxiety regarding homosexuality by turning to heterosexual activity. In Dream 5, he finds going out with a girl unsatisfactory, experiences being surrounded by large phallic figures, and loses control although he tries to "go straight."

In the morning, Don remembered the dreams in the order 5, 4, 2, 3, ending with the happy Paris dream. Like Jerry, he could not recall the first dream until reminded that it took place in a boardinghouse. In elaborating this dream, he revealed that he had just moved into the boardinghouse, his first time living away from home, and that it is "full of homosexuals." He feels that he really should move out, but housing close to school is hard to come by and he has no place to go. He has even thought of going back home to live with his father. He is clearly panicked by the threatening prospect of his present living arrangement; this is the other major element in Dream 1, along with his anxiety associated with being in a passive position as a sleep lab subject and with actively operating on a prone male in the gross anatomy lab. Living in the boardinghouse, like sleeping in the lab, puts him in a vulnerable position, and his first dream is continuous with his real-life situation: both involve being spied upon and open to physical attack. This reminds him in Dream 2 of feeling physically threatened by degenerate males in the past. In the morning, Don added that this incident actually happened: "I was once followed by men and I entered a drugstore and the pharmacist called the police and the police drove me home." This anxiety reaches such heights in Dream 2, which provides no rescue, that his next dream is one of pure escape. When he recalled this dream, he said it also had a basis in reality: "I just withdrew money from my bank account to go to France this summer." He recognizes in the dream that follows that escape is not the permanent solution to his sexual uneasiness. He dreams of "cooling it" with males and turning to heterosexual experiences. These all misfire, and he ends the night surrounded by masculine sex symbols and in trouble. In his morning recall, he ends up rejecting the girl of his last dream by saying: "As for the car, I've got my own car, so I don't need hers."

Don characterized Dreams 1 and 2 as "unpleasant." These were continuous with his waking experience. Dream 3, the Paris dream, was complementary to his current waking state; this he labeled "pleasant." Dream 4 was "neutral," and 5 "unpleasant." Clearly, the major theme of these dreams was not one to be handled in a nontherapeutic situation. For this reason, the subject was not encouraged to try to tie the material together. He understood that he was feeling very anxious about his living arrangement, and the discussion of this in relation to Dream 1 led him to the determination to move out of his present place. The dream-and-recall experience helped him pull some of these thoughts together and to mobilize himself to some productive action.

Just reading through these dream accounts, even without systematic dream analysis, leaves little doubt that there is meaning in each group. Both Jerry's and Don's dreams were at first continuous with what was on their minds prior to sleep. These were followed by dreams complementary in nature. As groups of dreams, they give us much insight into the inner lives of these two young men, particularly since only one night's dream data are involved. True, these were not typical nights in their lives. Sleeping in the laboratory seems to raise subjects' general level of anxiety, which makes other current anxiety themes available, by association, for dream production. These combined laboratory and private concerns appear in condensed and symbolic form in the early dreams. By the middle of the night, both subjects' dreams attempted to deal with this anxiety, one by regression, the other by fantasy escape. In both cases, also, these coping mechanisms appear to be inadequate. Jerry's and Don's final dreams of the night show that their areas of vulnerability still need to be resolved.

## The Nature of Dream Series

If Jerry's and Don's experiences are typical, the nature of a night's dream activity cannot be called random. Dreams begin with the feelings and concerns the person was experiencing just before sleep. Those that follow are related to the first, but are older examples of situations in which the same feelings are experienced. Not all dreams are concerned with the present and the past; some anticipate the future. Don's Paris dream not only is a wishful escape from the previous dream of being trapped in the drugstore, but represents what he has reason to anticipate in reality, having just withdrawn money for a summer trip to France.

Nighttime mental life, like daytime thought, is nevertheless mostly centered on the present. It is also, like waking thought, engaged in thinking forward and backward in time. We have the capacity in both states to recall the related past and to anticipate the way things may go in future. Of course, dreaming differs from daytime thought in many ways, one of which is in the relationship among elements. In dreams, associations are more emotional than logical, and the language is more imagistic and metaphoric than verbal and literal. These processes allow a lot of meaning to be packaged very economically, but really not all that mysteriously: having accounts of *all* the dreams of the night makes it easier to understand them, even without expert help, particularly because hunches about their meaning can be cross-validated from one dream to the next. In each of the two series reproduced above, the dreams appear to have an inherent logic in terms of their sequencing, to belong together as a group.

Jung urged that dreams be interpreted in a series rather than singly, arguing that this is the way to stay close to the data. Working with a group of dreams, recurrent themes can be recognized. With a single dream, the analyst becomes too dependent on the subject's waking associations to derive some meaning and allows the subject too much latitude to evade dream meanings.

Few studies have concentrated on dream series in the laboratory, and those few have found it hard to make generalizations (Rechtschaffen, Vogel, & Shaikun, 1963). Verdone (1965) reported that dreams of the first half of the night often deal with the most recent time period in the life of the dreamer, while in the last half there is a backward progression in time, followed by a return at the end of the night to recent times. Don's and Jerry's dreams are generally consistent with this pattern.

Kramer, Whitman, Baldridge, and Lansky (1964) identified two patterns of relationship among the dreams of the night. In one, there is an overall thematic progression from dream to dream, with an alternation between dreams with disturbing themes, in which tension is accumulating, and dreams involving reactions to the first kind, in which there is a discharge of tension. In the other pattern, no forward motion is discernible from dream to dream. Instead, there is a repetitive restatement of the same problem from one to the next. The dream series of both students conforms more closely to the first of these patterns, a progression over the night from the original problem statement.

In Jung's (1964) view, the general function of dreaming is *compensatory*, one of restoring the dreamer's psychological balance. Dreams arise to reestablish a psychological balance between the conscious and the unconscious. It is difficult to test this idea with only one night of dream data. The need for balancing may be stronger at some times— after a period of extreme self-denial, for example—than at other times. The laboratory, too, may impose additional difficulties. One problem difficult to avoid in the lab is that the dreamer is not allowed to finish each dream. He must be awakened before the REM period is over, otherwise recall may be lost. This procedure may itself keep tensions high. Another problem in the laboratory is that the subject is usually awakened at an arbitrary time in the morning, which may interrupt a natural series before it can be completed. Validating Jung's view might well require longer series, more nights, and much more information about the subject's daytime life. It would also be necessary to collect dreams under contrasting conditions: when the individual is upset, and thus in need of rebalancing, and when he is well functioning. In fact, the controversy over whether dreams are either complementary to or continuous with one's waking life may be based on too simplistic a notion. It may be that either or both types can be represented in a given series or set of series, their proportions depending on the dreamer's prevailing psychological balance. Frustrating daytime experiences might tend to produce dreams that are compensatory in content, while the dreams of persons with well-balanced waking functioning may be more continuous with daytime experiences. Most of the dreams Don and Jerry experienced in their nights in the lab were of the continous sort, but some were complementary to their waking state. On this basis, we might hypothesize that although these subjects have some areas of difficulty, they are in fairly good psychological shape.

We might summarize by saying that in a dream series, the first dreams appear to be related rather directly to present anxieties, the following dreams to emotionally associated experiences from the past, and the final ones to contemplated solutions. If this is a fair description of the process as it typically occurs, does the dream series ordinarily accomplish something? In a lab, because subjects are awakened at the time their dreams occur in order to recall them, rational processes enter the picture, possibly integrating the waking experience and the emotional response. Is there a comparable working over of emotion-laden material during the night, serving some regulatory function, when there is *no* awakening and *no* recall? Adlerians think so. "It is not necessary for the dream to be consciously recalled for it to do its work any more than it is necessary to consciously recall a decision in order for that decision to influence subsequent behavior" (Shulman, 1969, pp. 121–122). If, however, conscious awareness of the dream is necessary for dreaming to be beneficial, why is our memory of this material so very poor? Can it be improved with practice? Would such memory be helpful? These are the questions addressed in the next chapter.

# Three

# WHY ARE DREAMS
# SO HARD TO RECALL?

## Who Can and Who Cannot Remember
## Their Dreams

When people are asked how often and how well they remember their dreams, some reply that they recall their dreams in great detail and with a good deal of regularity, while others stoutly maintain, "I have never had a dream in my entire life." Most people fall somewhere between these two extremes and remember a dream or two a week. On the basis of the laboratory experience, we know that in fact all normal adults are experiencing four or five periods of REM sleep each night. This means that in a typical week less than 10 percent of the potential of thirty dreams will be recalled, and these rarely in much detail or for very long. If Don's and Jerry's dreams from their night of laboratory awakenings are a fair example of one night's products, these are a rich source of material, both for those working to understand the mind of man in general and for the individual's self-understanding. This makes the poverty of our unaided recall unfortunate. On learning how much they may be missing, many people ask: "How come?" and "What can I do about it?"

### Factors Affecting Recall

The question of why dreams are typically so poorly recalled is still something of a puzzle despite the great amount of attention paid to this problem since the 1950s. Work in the past decades has led to some advances in our understanding beyond Freud's general rule that dreams are repressed because they deal with material unacceptable to the waking mind. One thing is clear: the ability to recall our dreams is very much related to how we wake up and our prevailing motivation at the time. All we have to do to be convinced of this is to note how much more likely we are to recall a dream on mornings when we waken at leisure (on weekends, for example) than on a workday morning. The reason for this appears to be related to the simple fact that during the dream state our attention is fixed on internally generated images and that when we awaken we shift this focus to the outside world of sounds and sights. When a person is awakened in the lab at the time his EEG record shows that he is in the active REM state and is asked what was going through his mind, his first response is usually a vague demurrer: "Gee, I don't know . . . wait a minute . . . I think . . . oh, yes . . . I was . . ." and so on. In other words, it takes some effort after shifting out of sleep to shift back, search, and recapture the retreating dreams. Most often in the home situation, we have neither the time nor the incentive to do this backtracking once we have made the transition to the waking state. Usually at the moment of waking we are most concerned with turning off the alarm clock and getting on with our morning routine. It is only when we wake without these action-oriented pressures and can lie back a while and hover between sleep and waking that we are likely to recall what we were just experiencing.

Both Don and Jerry were about-average recallers of dreams under ordinary circumstances, but in the laboratory each recalled four of his five dreams without any prompting in the morning. This is evidence that once a dream has been consciously recollected during the night and translated into a verbal report, it is likely to be stored in memory in such a way that we can get to it again in the morning. It may be that this is the only way dreams can be recalled—that we must awaken and rehearse them. It is certainly true that we are more likely to remember the nightmare from which we awaken with heart pounding in the middle of the night than other, less exciting dreams; whether this is because of the exciting quality of the dream or because it woke us is hard to prove. Both of these factors seem to influence how well dreams are usually remembered. Persons monitored in the laboratory and awakened from each dream of the night most often remember the last dream best in the morning, and next most often they usually recall the first dream of the night. Don and Jerry were exceptions to the rule. Dreams that occur between the first and the last are less frequently recalled unless they happen to be particularly long or exciting (Meier, Ruef, Ziegler, & Hall, 1968; Trinder & Kramer, 1971). Being awakened from REM sleep helps recall, but it cannot guarantee complete recollection.

Can we recall an exciting middle-of-the-night dream in the morning if it did not waken us at the time? This is a very difficult question to answer. Often this seems the case—as when we recall more than one dream in the morning (only one of which could be the last one) and don't recall having awakened during the night to recall the other dream or dreams. Although this argument is logical, the EEG evidence shows that on nights when no experimental sleep interruptions are made, there are often very brief, spontaneous awakenings during or just at the end of a REM period. It appears that we lie still while watching the "dream movie" and then shift around or turn over at the start of another episode or at the end. This body movement is often accompanied by a short arousal from sleep. It may be that we take note of the dream during this aroused state and file it for morning recall, although we usually do not later remember that we were briefly awake.

Perhaps dreams that are immediately followed by NREM (non-REM) sleep are not recalled in the morning, because the brain state during NREM sleep is not conducive to transmitting the experiences of sleep into memory stores. One difference between the person who recalls his dreams well and the nonrecaller may be that the first typically awakes in the morning out of his last REM period (see Figure 1), while the second wakes up out of a NREM stage of sleep.

### Training Recall

Usually we have little or no particular incentive to recall our dreams. One exception is the person in psychotherapy who is requested by his therapist to discuss his dreams during treatment. If he obliges with one or more dreams per night, it is likely that, aside from his increased motivation, he has used some aids to record these—say, a bedside pad of paper or tape recorder. He may even train himself to wake at the end of REM intervals. This may sound surprising. How can we rouse ourselves out of sleep "to order," at just the right time to catch a dream? Actually, we have a good deal of control over our behavior during sleep when presumably we are inactive and unconscious. Certainly more than we usually recognize or ordinarily use. Mothers of very young children commonly awaken very quickly at their infant's first whimper, even though they may sleep through thunderstorms. Noises are only likely to wake us if they come from situations requiring us to actively respond. All of this implies that we can in fact make fine discriminations during sleep as to what is important.

Many people instruct themselves prior to sleep when to awaken and do so at specific times without an alarm clock. Even though these experiences are familiar to most of us, we still might question whether we can actually monitor our own internal behavior while asleep with sufficient accuracy to recognize, "Now I am dreaming," and then take the next step to recall, "I would like to remember this in the morning," and finally to rouse ourselves from sleep and write it all down. This seems like an enormous amount of awareness and control to take place during unconsciousness. Yet several research studies have shown not only that it is possible, but that subjects can be rather easily trained in the procedure.

In one study (Antrobus, Antrobus, & Fisher, 1965), student nurses were asked to signal the experimenter, as they slept, whenever they were aware that they were dreaming. This they did by closing a microswitch taped to one hand. Since this signal was recorded on the EEG record where their sleep stages were also being registered, their accuracy in identifying REM sleep could be directly checked. Without any external cues or any knowledge of the accuracy of their responses, all four subjects signaled that they were dreaming during REM sleep much more often than they signaled during NREM sleep. This study has been replicated and the results improved upon (Salamy, 1970) by adding a "punishment" for those who fail to signal. If subjects did not indicate that they were dreaming within the first three minutes of a REM period, they were awakened. With this stimulus as a reinforcement*, subjects quickly learned to make more correct responses. These studies show that it is possible while asleep to discriminate between dreams and other mental activity and to take action on the basis of this. By implication then, if we are motivated to recall our dreams, and if we set ourselves to this task before falling asleep, we can possibly split off some attention to monitor our internal experience and force ourselves to wake up and take note of this material when it occurs.

Several elements appear to be involved in whether or not we recall our dreams in the morning:

1. Our presleep intention. (More often our intention is to rest and forget the world than it is watch out for whatever dreams come by.)
2. The stage of sleep from which we awaken, REM or NREM.
3. The nature of the dreams themselves—their degree of excitement and length both influence their chances of being retained—as well as their serial position in the night.
4. How distracted we are when we wake up.

*An effect that serves to strengthen a response

5. How much sense they make to us and the context we have to relate them to.

6. The social importance given to dreams by persons we respect and the role of dreams in the culture generally.

### The Use of Dream Recall: Cultural Factors

Given all the right circumstances, then, the recall of dreams might well be increased. If, on top of that, we had some practice interpreting them or if we valued the opinion of people who argued for their significance, this might be useful for our daily waking lives as well. Certainly in the American majority culture dream recall is not encouraged. When a child wakes up from a bad dream, parents are likely to comfort him by saying: "It was *only* a dream. See, I'll put on the light and you can see it's not real. Just go back to sleep and forget it." If we are brave enough to continue to tell our dreams to others, our accounts are usually met with laughter at best, but more likely with boredom. Over time such reactions have a strongly discouraging effect.

The best evidence of how regular dream interpretation might affect the everyday lives of reasonably healthy people comes not from American society, where the concept is alien to us, but from studies of other cultures. One such account of a contemporary group in northern Malaya, the Senoi (Stewart, 1951), has raised some interest among the young in this country in this possibility (Greenleaf, 1973; Garfield, 1974). The Senoi believe that dreams represent accumulated tensions; Senoi children are taught that these tensions can only be dispelled by taking a positive attitude toward dreaming as a learning experience and are trained in using this experience daily to correct reality situations which gave rise to these pressures. Children report their dreams each morning at breakfast to the father, who listens acceptingly and gives each advice on how to handle the dream itself, so as not to be frightened if it should recur, and what to do to correct the reality situation which gave rise to that dream: give a present to your friend if you dream he is angry at you, for example.

Descriptions of how these people live emphasize the absence of the usual social problems. They have no war, no crime, and no mental illness, and so have no need for the institutions other cultures use to control these problems: they have no police, no jails, no army. Theirs is apparently a completely peaceful society, rich in creative products such as song, dance, poetry, and design. Their explanation for the flowering of their culture is that once the anxieties of childhood have been worked out in the way described above, their dreams become the source of artistic inspiration: these dreams are thus also translated into action on awakening, in the form of artistic contributions to the group. True the Senoi, who are taught that they have an obligation to work out their personal problems and a method for doing this by sharing their dreams, are poor in material possessions by Western standards and lack sophisticated technology. Yet we who are rich in these respects are poor in our sense of inner security and peace—and know little about regulating our internal world to our benefit.

The Senoi are not the only people who recall and interpret their dreams in a personally and socially functional way. Another study (Eggan, 1955) reports that the Hopi of Arizona also believe that bad dreams must be discussed immediately upon awakening in order to offset their bad effects. The Hopi, like the Senoi, enjoy a peaceful, democratic way of life characterized by honesty and cooperativeness.

D'Andrade (1961) reasoned that dreams will be assigned an important role in any culture, under certain conditions: a cultural requirement that young adults survive on their own, a high degree of personal anxiety over being in this situation, and a lack of external supports and resources available to make survival on one's own feasible. Under these conditions, he argued, internal, fantasized means of getting control of resources, such as dreams, become important. For example, in fifty-seven cultures that he reviewed, he found that those where young men were required to leave their familiar villages when they married also used dreams to control the supernatural. In sixty-three cultures he found a highly significant association between the degree of emphasis on dreams and the type of economy: dreams were viewed as important in those societies which had a risky economy based on hunting and fishing more often than in those based on a more stable agricultural economy. When anxiety over personal survival is high, where survival is difficult, but the value on self-reliance is also high, D'Andrade maintained, dreams become a source of power to gain a greater sense of control over one's life situation.

Dream recall for both Senoi children and the groups surveyed by D'Andrade is related to inner tension, anxiety, and a sense of self-responsibility for working these out. Does this help to explain differences in the ability to recall dreams between individuals in our own culture? Perhaps it accounts in part for the general increase of interest in dreams among young people today. Certainly the economy has become more risky since the 1960s, while traditional mutual support among family members has lessened. This makes the young eager to search out other resources for increasing their insight into the world and so gaining more control over their lives.

## Personality and Dream Recall

Although many personality characteristics have been investigated in relation to the ability to recall dreams, only two have been found to have even tenuous associations. Those two associations give some support to the anthropological findings such as D'Andrade's. One trait that good dream recallers seem to share is anxiety, and the other is something that has been called, variously, inner acceptance, field independence, internal control, and introtensiveness — all terms that refer to an awareness of, interest in, or reliance on our own experience, in contrast to being dependent on how others define things or on the external context of situations to shape our views.

Thus people reporting that they have high recall of their dreams at home usually have higher test scores on measures of anxiety than those who report low home recall (Schonbar, 1965; Tart, 1962). They are also people who pay more attention to their inner feelings and responses (Lewis, Goodenough, Shapiro, & Sleser, 1966).

Laboratory studies of sleep have shown that REM sleep, like anxiety, is characteristically a state of high cerebral arousal. The brain wave pattern is very similar to that of alert wakefulness in frequency and amplitude (see Figure 2). The heart rate, pulse, and respiration are irregular. There are rapid conjugate movements of the eyes, and, in the male, penile erections synchronous with the change to this EEG pattern every ninety minutes, and a profound loss of muscle tonus in the head and neck. This does not sound like a very restful state, particularly when we contrast it with the situation in NREM sleep, where brain waves, heart rate, pulse, and respiration are all slowed down and more regular, the eyes do not move, and the penis is flaccid. It is possible that the REM sleep of some more generally anxious individuals is even more highly agitated than the average and that these are the people who typically have higher dream recall. It is also possible that when those who ordinarily sleep well are in a period of anxiety they sleep less soundly and so recall more dreams at these times. If, when we are upset, our dreams also have a more dramatic flavor, then it is more likely still that under these circumstances they will be more easily recalled.

Some of this speculation has been confirmed by laboratory study (Snyder, 1960; Goodenough, Lewis, Shapiro, & Sleser, 1965). Using the amount of sound stimulation that it takes to waken a sleeper as an indication of the depth of his sleep, it has been found that the less sound it takes to awaken the subject from REM,* the more likely he is to recall his dream. When subjects remembered a dream, it took 20 decibels less to wake them than when they failed to remember dreaming.

In another study (Zimmerman, 1970), very light sleepers—those easier to wake from *all* of their sleep stages—were found to differ from very deep sleepers in that they reported dreams even when awakened from NREM stages of sleep. Dreaming may be a kind of mental activity which is constantly ongoing during sleep, but which we only become aware of when the arousal level is high and we are not attending to external affairs. For most people, this is the situation that occurs in REM. To be able to recall this experience requires that the brain activation level be even higher, as happens when we wake up.

This may account for why some deep sleepers who have little or no dream recall in their familiar beds at home can come into a sleep laboratory and recall four or five dreams in a single night. Just sleeping under these circumstances is a sufficiently unusual experience to arouse some anxiety. This makes the first few nights of laboratory sleep lighter than usual. It is typically a more alert and less restful sleep, with longer initial periods of time lying awake before sleep comes, and longer intervals before sleep can be regained after an awakening is made. This is bad for sleep but good for dream recall.

### Helping the Poor Recaller

Given what we know about the memory for dreams, can we increase it? Can we train a poor dream recaller to become a good one? If we set the expectations that the sleeper will remember his dreams, awaken him in the laboratory in the appropriate sleep stages, and have him talk the material over with an interested, knowledgeable person in the morning, will we heighten his awareness of dreaming sufficiently to affect his degree of spontaneous recall?

We tested this with twenty-eight poor dream recallers, fourteen of each sex. They all slept in the laboratory for eight successive nights. On the first two nights, they were not awakened until morning, when they were asked if they remembered anything of their dreams. For the next four nights half were given help in recalling dreams by being awakened during each REM period and questioned about the details. The other half were awakened as often, but only from NREM sleep. Each morning, after they

*REM *sleep* is commonly referred to simply as *REM*.

got up and dressed, all the subjects' reports from that night were reviewed with them and they were encouraged to think about their dreams and to look for patterns of relationships among them. For the last two lab nights, they slept again without any interruption, to check whether they could remember their dreams without help any better than previously. In contrast to the first morning, when fifteen remembered nothing, on the last morning only seven had no recall. However, both groups gained in ability. Perhaps just the attention and the knowledge that they were expected to recall dreams were enough to help to some extent. This led us to wonder whether longer training might be more specifically effective. Let's look at a specific example.

## LIZ AND KEN: A GOOD AND A POOR RECALLER

We had a chance to test this possibility when Liz, a young married student with unusually high recall of her home dreams, agreed to sleep in the laboratory for a night of dream collections once a month over a six-month period. Her husband, Ken, did not want her to travel to the university alone at night and so planned to accompany her. We asked if he would not like to participate in the study also, sleeping in the laboratory on those nights. He explained that this would be a waste of our time as he had not recalled a dream since he was a child. We assured him that it was quite all right with us whether or not he had any dreams to report. No awakenings were made their first night, while they were getting used to the procedures and comfortable with the experimenters. On the second night, both Liz and Ken were awakened four times, once in each of their REM periods. Each time, Liz gave a long, detailed dream report, often with several episodes and several changes of scene and characters. In the morning, she fully recalled all of these dreams and was able to make numerous associations to them. Ken could recall dreams only on three awakenings. Although his reports of them were very brief, only two or three sentences in length, he was delighted in the morning to find he remembered them at all.

Ken was a graduate student in art, stocky in build, with a flowing mustache, a self-assured manner, and a dry wit. He loved to collect and trade old cars and musical instruments. In his own words, he was "clever, skeptical, independent, self-centered, and confident; a doer, not a thinker." Liz came from a large Catholic family in a small community. She was in her last year of an undergraduate social science program, frail-looking, a bit defiant and very insecure, looking younger than her twenty-two years. She described herself as naive, spontaneous, narcissistic, but worried and preoccupied with herself.

These two had been married a year at the time of the study. They had decided not to have children for awhile, which created some internal problems for Liz because of her family's expectations. Ken and Liz instead turned her dog, Brutus, into something of a baby-substitute. Since these two had lived through many experiences together and shared many of their waking hours, it seemed a good opportunity to study the differences between a good and a poor dream recaller and their dream responses to the same situation. Particularly, it was a chance to investigate whether the level of recall changes with practice and whether it is higher after anxiety-arousing experiences. Would Ken produce more exciting and more memorable dreams after a particularly bad day?

Once a week they each took a number of psychological tests, including a test of anxiety (Spielberger, Gorsuch, & Lushene, 1969), in addition to the monthly night of dream collections. The anxiety test confirmed that Liz was more anxious than Ken. On another test measuring their degree of mood disturbance for the previous week (McNair, Lorr, & Droppleman, 1971), Ken appeared to be very calm and stable in his moods. In terms of the norms for university students his age, his mood disturbance level was very low. Liz, on the other hand, scored extremely high on this test. Ken scored below average on tests for levels of tension, depression, anger, and confusion throughout the study, while Liz's scores were well above average on all but two of the months. The impression Ken gave, of someone who was much more at peace with himself than was his wife, was confirmed in all the tests and interviews and by his dreams.

Throughout the study period Ken usually had a dream to report on all but one of his awakenings from his REM periods. Usually he came up blank on his first or second REM period of the night. Liz, on the other hand, never failed to recall a dream when she was awakened. In the morning, Ken always had trouble remembering his dreams and had to be prompted frequently. He had even more difficulty making sense out of his dreams and connecting them in any way to his present or past life, while Liz could hardly be persuaded to stop. In general, her high-level and his low-level dream production remained the same throughout the study period.

The opportunity to test whether Ken's performance would change if he were under stress came on the fourth month of the study. Ken and Liz arrived at the lab that night rather upset. They were facing a critical decision in their lives. Both were due to finish their degree programs and were beginning to think about what was to come next. Liz wanted to go to graduate school wherever she could get accepted. And while Ken, as an artist, could live anywhere, this arrangement would involve a certain reversal in their roles: she would take the lead in determining where they would live, and he would follow. This was definitely not his style. On the night in question, both hit their highest level on the anxiety test and the highest mood disturbance levels, although Ken was still very low in relation to Liz. During his presleep interview, Ken reported that there were three things on his mind:

> I was thinking about my wife getting into graduate school. I am doing everything I can to help, which, of course, is little. (*Question: Do you want her to go?*) I can't do very much to help. She was figuring [her grade point average] and got very anxious. (*Question: A lot depends on her Graduate Record Exam, then?*) Right. She's very blown out over the whole thing. I'm thinking of writing a letter of protest. . . .
>
> (*Question: How have you been feeling during the day?*) Lately, very, very anxious. Because of all I've got to do. I've got a Spanish test to take. I studied hard, and if there is a God in heaven, I *should* pass.
>
> I have a wall tonight [in the lab bedroom], that's great. (*Question: You like the wall?*) Liz and I have big fights over walls. That's the only way I can sleep, at the edge of the bed and leave the rest to Liz. Otherwise she pushes me off the bed. I hate that. Now the dog sleeps on the bed. There's no room for me in the bed anymore. The stupid dog. . . .

All three of these areas of irritation appeared in his dreams: helping his wife during her anxiety over getting into graduate school, while feeling somewhat antagonistic about it and rather impotent; feeling pressured to get everything done satisfactorily to complete his own degree and being unsure of how his work will be judged; and anger at the role of the dog as the indulged baby of their household who displaces him. The dream reports were very short, and he was more ineffective than ever working with this material productively in the morning. As he recounted in these dreams:

> It had something to do with cars, I don't remember what . . . either being somewhere on time or taking someone's place doing something. That's about all.
>
> *Possible theme: time pressure to get things done and changing places with Liz with respect to who's in the driver's seat.*
>
> Liz and I were talking about being able to start this car. It was a big sedan, fairly old, like a '40s or '50s. It was part of a game show where you had to find a very important part of an old car, and if you found the part, like the key, and you got the object to work, you got the car. I think Liz was in the show and I was kinda her assistant, one way or another.

*Possible theme: it is my role now to help Liz get going on her own, to win her own mobility.*

I got a sponge from the sink in the ceramics studio and I wetted it so I wouldn't burn my hand if I went to take a lid off a hot kiln. I was just ready to put the sponge on the handle when you woke me. Liz was in [the dream]. She was kinda helping me.

*Possible theme: I know how to protect myself when things get too hot to handle within my own sphere, if Liz is in her proper place.*

Ken reported two more dreams that night. In the fourth one, he is walking the dog in a park and the dog tries to defecate in the middle of the path. He attempts to drag the dog away so he won't be embarrassed by this, since he is being observed by another young man who is walking a well-behaved dog. In the last dream of the night, a woman student in the studio asks him to run an errand for her, to get her some milk. He refuses, saying that he is busy and she has two legs and should go herself. He is scolded for this by his instructor, but adamantly maintains that this girl is expecting too much.

Within these short dreams, Ken expresses the need to take care of himself at this time, while also feeling a sense of pressure to help Liz take on more of an active role, to help her find the key to winning in the graduate school game. This leads to an awareness that he must protect himself and be careful in taking the lid off this hot situation, and that Liz should help him keep cool. His impatience with the dog-baby and with Liz's expecting too much care and feeding from him comes to a head in the last two dreams in which he expresses his anger (chastising the dog and arguing with the instructor).

In the morning, when asked if he had any idea how these dreams might relate to what was on his mind the night before, Ken replied, "No. Do you?" He was then asked, "What was your general underlying feeling throughout these dreams?" and he replied, "Pissed off. Not in the kiln dream, but definitely in the last dream and the dog dream. The first one was short and the second one I can't relate to. I don't understand it."

In contrast, Liz's dreams on this night were extremely long, the reports running to twenty typed pages. She picked up the same themes, but handled them in a much more complicated, metaphorical way, involving many more family relationships and future possibilities. The graduate school dilemma she resolved in a dream of escaping to a simple country life with Ken in a cabin in the woods filled with pots of his making and far away from the hassles of the city. However, reality catches up with them in the form of a major traffic jam with cars crashing into their retreat. In her dream, Ken urges her to pay for the damage.

The second theme she deals with is their dog situation and her embarrassment at her emotional attachment to such a messy, bothersome, socially unacceptable creature. In the third, she recognizes Ken's fascination with old cars and her insecurity about her femininity and attractiveness to Ken but her appreciation of his caring for her.

Ken was not a highly verbal person; he was an artist. In his work, he dealt in visual images and manipulated materials to express these directly in physical forms. All of this is activity associated with the right hemisphere of the brain. His night dreams were short, direct, and easy to understand. Yet he always had difficulty dealing with these verbally. His dreams did not get longer, nor did his recall of them improve much with practice. Liz, too, came into and went out of the study much the same. She consistently had long dreams with detailed recall and multiple associations. She was constantly intrigued by her dreams and worked hard at uncovering their meanings. Perhaps Ken was one of those lucky people who is like a good Senoi or, in Jung's terms, living a well-balanced life, at peace with himself, so that his dreams did not often need to deal with much inner tension material. Perhaps he related to his inner fantasies and reconciled them with reality during the daytime through his art.

Part of Ken's graduation was an exhibition of his work. The pieces on display were large abstract sculptures, often phallic in shape, decorated with parts of old cars. They were lovely fantasies, all in shiny pastel colors —his waking dreams, an embodiment of his emotional concerns in palpable forms.

Liz's waking life was one in which verbal intellectual activity predominated. She read and wrote and manipulated concepts, all functions which are controlled by the brain's left hemisphere. She had little room for focusing on fantasy until nightfall. She dreamed in complicated symbolic images and used her recall of these to enrich her waking life. Ken worked by day to fashion real things to represent his personal response to his reality in visual-spatial terms. He had difficulty with verbal tasks. Because of his inability to learn Spanish he almost flunked out of school. His dreams were perhaps less elaborate and more straightforward because he had less need to compensate for an unbalanced day. Despite all the aids of the laboratory and their own fluctuations in anxiety level, Ken and Liz showed characteristic differences in dreaming and recall which seem to relate to their more stable waking lifestyle, and probably also to the ways their waking attention was being engaged.

The laboratory can be useful in facilitating access to dream data but does not improve the level of spontaneous recall very much. This alone does not change the particular nature of dreams or the function they serve. These factors seem to be more intimately tied up with long-term personality patterns; and may be best approached as part of a twenty-four-hour psychology. How do the dreams fit into the day before and day after? If the ways our minds work in dreaming and in waking states are interdependent, can we learn more about dream function by shifting the existing balance to increase or decrease the amount of dream experience? Such a strategy might help to reveal whether unrecalled dreams have some necessary role, as we examine the effects of their absence or intensification on the behavior that follows.

Four

# EXPLORING DREAM FUNCTION

## I. Where Do Dreams Go
## When REM Is Removed?

As we have seen in the preceding chapter, despite the fact that dreaming is both regular and plentiful, most people find their unaided recall is quite irregular and minimal. Imagine the surprise of a poor dream recaller like Ken when he finds that an underground movie house has been playing four or five Theater of the Absurd versions of "This Is Your Life" every night behind his back. Not only does a good deal of dreaming typically go on unnoticed, but as a whole it appears to have inherent meaning that is directly relevant to the waking concerns of the dreamer.

Finding that we can make sense of a group of dreams once we become aware of them does not necessarily mean that they regularly perform a useful function. On the other hand, consciousness may not be necessary for dreams to do their work. Many of our other processes actually work best without our paying any attention to them. Both respiration and digestion, for instance, operate outside of consciousness most of the time, the exception being when they are acting up. This may also be true of dreaming, since we seem to be most aware of it when we are most anxious and sleeping least well. Remembering a dream, then, may indicate that its ordinary function is not operating at its optimum.

Jung was quite explicit about this. He believed that the mind has a self-regulating capacity through compensation. In dreams, the unconscious supplies all the material related to some present situation which is necessary for a complete adaptation to the problem. Under normal circumstances, this works unconsciously. Only in the neurotic is the contrast between what we are aware of and what we are not so marked that this automatic compensation cannot take place. This kind of formulation was hard to prove or disprove until recent improvements in methods of studying dreams.

### Effects of REM Reduction: Natural

One way to reveal the role of a component in a functioning whole is the "surgical method"—finding out what happens or fails to happen when we remove the component. This method has been applied to discover something about the "why" of dreaming. The surgery in this instance involves removing the stage of sleep most closely associated with dreaming. This is done by waking the person each time he enters the REM sleep stage. Unfortunately, this method rests on an assumption which is false: that preventing REM sleep will prevent dreaming. True, the signs of REM sleep have proved to be quite reliable indicators that dreaming is taking place: 85 percent of the times that lab subjects are awakened from REM they report a dream in progress, while dreams are reported from other sleep stages less frequently and more sporadically. Yet it is also true that we may be able to remove the surface indicators of the dream — that is, prevent REM—but not stop the dreaming process itself. Leaving this problem aside temporarily and assuming that we can prevent most, if not all, dreaming in this way, what are the consequences of experiencing less than our normal amount of dreaming?

Sometimes there is a natural loss of REM sleep time when, for one reason or another, we are awake when we should be sleeping. We could look into the effects of this on the next day's behavior, if it were not that this surgery is too major: any effects of REM loss would be confused with the loss of all the other stages of sleep as well.

We need to find circumstances under which REM sleep is reduced while total sleep time remains intact. This is the case following the ingestion of certain drugs. Many tranquilizers, barbiturates, hypnotics, antidepressants, and antihistamines cut down the proportion of REM in the night's sleep. In fact, almost anything that an insomniac might take to help him sleep "better," including a couple of stiff drinks, will, if effective at all, help him sleep "deeper," with more NREM and less REM than normal (Oswald, 1969). What is more, this sleep is not necessarily more restful. Usually, such a night has more of the lightest of the NREM sleep stages, Stage 2, and less of the very quiet delta sleep, Stages 3 and 4 (see Figure 2). Often, too, such a sleep is punctuated with more than an average number of arousals. After a night like this, the person may have slept six or eight hours, but wakes feeling grouchy, groggy, and thick-headed, rather than bright, alert, and rested. Here again, we cannot be sure that these effects are due to the reduction of dreaming, since the presence of the drug makes it hard to tell which effects are due to which departure from the normal situation.

Nevertheless, both reduction in total sleep and the ingestion of certain drugs, because they result in a reduction of REM, are useful circumstances for providing clues to the effect of this loss on the next day's (and night's) behavior. One such consequence appears to be a change in normal sleep patterns. Whenever a person experiences a loss of sleep, either overall or of a specific stage, his sleep pattern subsequently shifts to compensate for this loss. If he has lost an entire night's sleep, for example, the next night he will have a prolonged period of quiet sleep and a delay before REM sleep appears. This shows that the deepest sleep, Stages 3 and 4, need to be recouped first and that REM sleep is of a second order of importance (Webb & Agnew, 1965). REM will also be increased, but this may not happen until the second night after a sleepless night. Whatever REM sleep does in terms of maintenance of health and welfare, it appears to be less vital than delta sleep.

Other evidence of the effects of REM loss comes from studies of persons who are withdrawing from sleeping medication. After a prolonged period of drug dependency, the first night or two of sleep without drugs may be accompanied by nightmares of frightening intensity. These can be so fearful that the person resumes taking pills rather than go through the horrors of withdrawal. Brain wave records in these cases show that REM not only increases in extent, but also in level of activity going on within it. The rapid movements of the eyes occur more frequently as the dream imagery becomes more fantastic and emotion-laden, as if too much dream material were being compressed into the time allotted to it (Oswald, 1969).

These reports of the effects of natural and drug-induced sleep loss, suggest that both the quiet delta and active REM sleep may be necessary for normal functioning, but they serve different needs—the first type may aid our physical rest and recuperation, a sort of time out to recover our strength before getting up and back into the game, and the second may supply a period during which our emotional responses to our experiences are reviewed and defused, a time to integrate new experience with the old before going on to add more. If this is a reasonable hypothesis about the function of dreams, does the removal of necessary REM force dreaming to invade other territories? Will the internal "studios" then be set up to produce dreams in other kinds of sleep or even during waking hours? And if this function does not occur, will waking behavior suffer, and if so, how?

## *Effects of REM Reduction: Experimental*

William Dement, who pioneered so much of current sleep research, was also the first to explore the effects of REM sleep loss in the laboratory by pinpointing specific sleep periods and aborting them by waking the sleepers to prevent dreaming. He found that if he wakened his subjects and kept them awake for at least three minutes every time they attempted to enter the REM state, they would not pick up the cycle where they left off when they returned to sleep. They would, instead, miss that REM period and start over with another descent into NREM sleep (see Figure 1).

In his first study of this kind (Dement, 1960), this routine was kept up for several nights, with several awakenings each night at the first signs of REM. Following this phase of the study, the subjects were allowed to sleep through the night for the next two nights. In order to provide a "control" —that is, to be sure that any effects noted were due specifically to the loss of REM and not just to the loss of sleep—the subjects slept in the lab again for a series of nights, this time having their NREM sleep interrupted as often as their REM sleep had been previously. This period was also followed by two "recovery" nights of normal sleep. The results were clear. The recovery nights looked quite different after the two types of sleep loss. Even the first night REM was interrupted, subjects began to act as if they had "missed" their dreams: the length of the sleep cycle became shorter. This meant that awakenings had to be made more frequently than once every ninety minutes if sleepers were to be kept out of REM sleep. Other experimenters who have used this method (Kales, Hoedemaker, Jacobson, & Lichtenstein, 1964; Sampson, 1965) confirm that it takes ten to twelve awakenings to keep REM from occurring on a first night of REM deprivation. The number varies a good deal from person to person, some sleepers needing as few as three, others as many as twenty-five awakenings. If REM deprivation is continued beyond one night, the number tends to climb from night to night, although here again the differences between subjects are marked: some show a sharp rise in the number of times they need to be awakened from night to night, and others level off after the first night.

Both subjects and experimenters come to hate this routine, as it often turns into a battle between them. The subjects' sleep records look as if they are trying more and more insistently to get into REM the longer researchers prevent it. Both sides wind up the night worn out from the effort and with a great respect for the possibility that there is a "need to dream," or at least a need for REM sleep.

Not only does the cycling between NREM to REM speed up, but usually subjects also change regarding how easily they awaken. Some become harder and harder to arouse from this sleep, and some wake up more easily. Everyone usually responds on the first night to a voice calling their name over an intercom. After that, those who are harder to awaken require both a call and the light being turned on in their bedroom. This, too, may fail after a while; the experimenter then must enter the room and shake the subject awake before he reluctantly leaves the REM. In some stubborn cases, not even this works after a night or two of no REM sleep. Then the subject must be hoisted onto his feet before his eyes stop their characteristic rapid darting movements which gave the name to this game. Those who become easier to awaken as deprivation proceeds seem to be in a lighter-than-usual sleep throughout the night. They report feeling that they are only resting while awaiting the next awakening. It is my impression that whatever the subject's usual sleep style, this becomes more pronounced under the stress of being constantly awakened. Deep sleepers become deeper sleepers, light sleepers become even lighter ones.

What happens at the end of these experimental nights when uninterrupted sleep is allowed again? For one thing, the first REM period of the night appears sooner, as if ninety minutes were too long to wait; also this first REM period will last longer than a usual first REM period. The most dramatic finding was that over the whole night, most subjects experience much more REM sleep than their normal amount, as though some compensation were needed for the amount lost. Note, however, that throughout this entire discussion nothing has been said about dreaming, only about REMing. What happens to dreaming when REM sleep is removed is another question.

When early work in REM deprivation made it appear to be a general law that REM loss must be made up subsequently, the search began to determine which aspects of REM are crucial and why. Is it the psysiological properties of this special kind of sleep that we need, or the psychological aspects of dreams, or both? Perhaps we simply need physical exercise, periodic physical reactivation to keep our bodies in good working order during the long night. To test this, Vogel (Vogel, Giesler, & Barrowclough 1970) had subjects get up and walk around the room a little every time a REM period was due to see if this activity would be an acceptable substitute for REM sleep. If this were the case, no REM deficit would accumulate, and so no later increase in REM time would take place. No such luck.

Perhaps it is the psychological opportunity to fulfill a wish. If so, maybe the overt gratification of a wish instead of a REM interval would suffice. Dement (1974) tells an amusing story of an attempt to test this hypothesis. He and Charles Fisher wondered whether a good substitute behavior for REM would be eating a favorite food. The subject for this trial run told them his favorite food was banana cream pie. Mrs. Fisher baked the pie. Each time the subject attempted to enter a REM period, he was awakened and given a piece of banana cream pie before being allowed to go back to sleep. The first three awakenings and pie eating sessions went fine. At the fourth awakening, the subject recalled a fragment of a dream that occurred just before he was wakened: "I was having a cup of coffee and a cigarette. I always have a cup of coffee and a cigarette at the *end* of a meal." On the fifth awakening, he recalled having started another dream: "I was given some spaghetti, but I was scraping it off the plate into a garbage can." The sixth time he was awakened, he reported, "Dr. Dement, I dreamed that I was feeding *you* banana cream pie." Clearly, the pie did not stop the dreaming; in fact, the need to stop eating became a dream theme of its own.

In the early work of the 1950s, there was no real check on subjects' mental life during other sleep stages (those that were not being suppressed), nor on the intervening waking hours between "dream deprivation" nights. It was assumed that no REM time meant no dreams; that dreams were a by-product of the activated brain state provided by REM sleep. However, although it is true to say "we dream when we REM," that does not mean the same as "we REM when we dream," as Lewis Carroll might put it. Foulkes (1962) was the first to explore the mental content in all sleep stages. He found that some dreaming does take place in NREM sleep, and, as we have noted before, this is especially true of the light sleeper. Since some people respond to REM deprivation by sleeping more lightly, perhaps they intensify their NREM dreaming.

In general the absence of REM at night did not seem to be followed by disorder and chaos during the day. There were no instances from the Dement (1960), Kales et al. (1964), and Sampson (1965) studies of "Dr. Jekylls" turning into "Mr. Hydes" as a result, nor were there any reports of dreams intruding into waking life causing normal people to behave like hallucinating psychotics, at least not after a few nights of REM loss. The effects on daytime behavior were, for the most part, minor; at worst, there were some reports of transitory unconventional thoughts and behaviors, and at best some increase in waking creativity. The worst was reported by Dement (1960), who noted that one of his subjects became rather paranoid and suspicious for a while. Another subject tried to cheat a waitress on a check for some drinks, behavior most uncharacteristic of him. The change for the better was reported informally by Kales in another study where, between lab nights, the two subjects spent their waking time on a hospital ward, even though they were perfectly well, in order that they could be watched to make sure they did not nap during the day. They filled their waking hours with leisure activities, mostly writing and painting. In the experimenter's judgment, both subjects produced more interesting creative work during this period than when they were sleeping normally.

Both of the above studies reported that REM-deprived subjects seem to become loosened up in their daytime behavior—what could be described as less conventional and conforming and more expressive of themselves. Does this mean that dreams operate as nightly safety valves so that we can act civilized during the day? If we are deprived of not just a few nights, but for long periods of time, might we become progressively less socially responsible, more lawless creatures, willing to do anything for its momentary pleasure value? Are there any examples of people who have lived without their dreams for extended periods of time which might give us clues to the effects of long-term REM abstinence on waking behavior?

At present, there is only tentative evidence. We know, for example, that alcohol suppresses REM sleep somewhat. The chronic alcoholic is thus someone who has accumulated a long-range REM deficit. We also know that the sudden withdrawal of alcohol is followed by delirium tremens ("DTs"). These are characterized by rather frightening visual hallucinations by day and an almost continuous REM sleep during the night (Greenberg & Pearlman, 1967; Gross, Goodenough, Tobin, Halpert, Lepore, Pearlstein, Sirota, DiBianco, Fuller, & Kishner, 1966). Alcoholism is often described in terms of unconventional, self-indulgent behavior, the same qualities which appear in a transitory fashion in the experimentally REM-deprived subject. It may be an overstatement to say that REM suppression is the major cause of this behavior in the alcoholic, but it should be noted as another correlation. Another observation of value comes from animal studies. There are ethical and practical considerations which limit the amount of REM loss imposed on normal humans to a few nights. With animals, REM suppression can be extended for longer times. Cats and rats which have been severely REM-deprived have been reported to show increased appetites and to become hypersexual (Dement, 1969). Cats, ordinarily fastidious creatures, will mount almost any animal, dead or alive,

male or female, sick or well, after sufficient REM deprivation. This instinctual drive becomes heightened (in terms of the amount of time it occupies) and loses all the refinements of its expression. From this evidence,
it looks as if REM routinely serves some discharge function for our basic
drives, and without it, watch out!

There is one group of people for whom such an effect would be an im-
provement in their waking lives: the chronically depressed. These people
lose interest in eating, in sex, and slow down generally in their activity
level. Vogel and his co-workers (Vogel, Thurmond, Gibbons, Sloan, Boyd,
& Walker, 1975) REM-deprived thirty-four seriously depressed patients in
a carefully controlled study for a long period of time. They report that half
the group improved enough with this treatment alone to be discharged
from the hospital without drugs or shock treatment having been used.
That with an average of seven weeks of REM deprivation half the patients
recovered is impressive, but for what is most intriguing in terms of dreams
is the fact that none of the patients treated this way became worse (Vogel,
1975).

## Is REM Deprivation Dream Deprivation?

Before we apply what we know about the effects of REM sleep loss to
deduce something about the function of dreams, we must first make sure
that dreams are really cut off by this maneuver. After all, perhaps the
dreams have only moved out of REM and taken up residence in some other
stage of sleep. When we considered some of the differences between how
well different people recall their dreams, we noted that very light sleepers
report dreaming whenever they are awakened. In fact, they appear to
dream as often in NREM as in REM. Knowing, too, that REM deprivation
lightens the sleep of some people suggests that dreaming not only *can* take
place in other sleep besides REM, but that more probably *does* when REM
is removed. The idea that dreaming is a kind of mental processing which is
going on at a low level all the time was proposed by Jung (1968, p. 87). We
become aware of this only when conditions are right: when our attention is
not deluged by external stimuli, our need to make active responses is
reduced, and yet the brain is in a state of activation. All of this occurs normally in REM, when sense receptors are turned down, muscle tone is
reduced, and the electrical energy of brain cells increases. If dreaming in
fact continuously goes on in the background, possibly the frequent
awakenings of the REM-deprivation routine increase the activation of the
brain enough to allow dreaming to cross the threshold of awareness in

sleep other than REM. This possibility should be explored before interpreting the effects of REM loss as the effects of dream loss.

Another possibility, if we in fact need to dream, is that when the lab subject is awakened as he attempts to enter REM, some kind of dreamlike activity intrudes into these waking periods. If the sleeper can indulge in a vivid fantasy every time we awaken him, this could explain the absence of any dramatic change in his morning behavior. In that case, we might too hastily conclude that dreams have no function—only because our dream surgery was a failure.

Both these possible sources of error need to be checked. We need to determine, under conditions of REM deprivation, (1) whether dreaming increases in NREM or preREM sleep and (2) what happens during waking intervals.

Ordinarily, the kind of dream reported varies a good deal from one REM awakening to the next, depending on the degree of physiological activity at the moment of awakening. If the sleeper is awakened during a burst of rapid eye movements and if many of these have taken place shortly beforehand, the dream is more likely to be an exciting one and the recall of it greater (Goodenough et al., 1965; Berger & Oswald, 1962). Also, the more rapid and irregular the breathing during the REM state, the more intense will be the reported dream (Hobson, Goldfrank, & Snyder, 1965). Some REM periods look quieter than others. The experimenter watching rather sparse eye movements and quiet, regular breathing anticipates a dull dream report. Awakenings at these times in fact produce blander dream reports or reports that no dreaming at all was taking place. When REM is experimentally suppressed, some people show an intensification of the sporadic eye activities just at the onset of the REM state. These seem to coincide with vivid dream imagery taking place in the brief moment before the awakening can be made. Subjects who respond in this way have increasingly more dreamlike reports as deprivation awakenings progress. Some dreaming, by taking evasive action, eludes the experimenter's best efforts to prevent it.

### REM Onset Fantasy

In one of the early deprivation studies carried out in our laboratory (Cartwright, Monroe, & Palmer, 1967), we had a chance to look into both the questions just posed. Subjects were awakened for three nights. We succeeded in reducing their proportion of REM sleep from an average of 24 percent before deprivation to 3 percent on the first deprivation night, 6 percent on Night 2, and 7 percent on Night 3. Despite this severe loss, only some subjects showed the expected increase in REM time on the following two nights of recovery sleep. Those who showed no recovery of their lost REM time on recovery nights had shown, on deprivation nights, the intensified eye movements discussed above just before they had been awakened to abort the REM; these sleepers had reported a good deal of dream material on each of these awakenings. This response we called the *substitution pattern* because there seemed to be an immediate increase in preREM sleep fantasy which functioned to substitute for the suppressed REM. Both Jerry and Don, whose dreams were reported in Chapter 2, were "substitutors," responding to this REM-deprivation experiment in this way. Even though their participation in the REM-deprivation study took place a year after their first night of dream collections, their recall of what was going through their minds when they were awakened sounded very familiar.

The first time Jerry was awakened on his first night of deprivation, he had no recall of any content. On his second awakening, he reported:

> I was doing algebra. I was in a small schoolhouse and seemed to be up at the blackboard doing algebra. I don't know why because I didn't seem to be very old at the time, maybe eight or nine years of age. It was a small schoolroom and a few kids here and there in the class. The main thing about the whole scene seemed to be me up at the blackboard scribbling away.

This has all the qualities of a dream. It is visual. He thinks he is really there. There is a distortion (of age). Here is Jerry, in his familiar country-boy role, struggling to do a task too big for him and feeling too immature to handle it. This is just like the dream he had when he was struggling to insert the plug from his electrodes into the right holes.

Don's reports upon awakening at the onset of REM were also very much like his dreams of the previous year. This one occurred on his second night of deprivation:

> I was a male nurse. I don't have much recollection of it except that there was a big stack of books that I had to read and a uniform that I had to wear and then I knew that I had to report the next day to this doctor. Various people came in and stole all the books or borrowed them, and the man from the library said he didn't know what to do but wait around all night until they started coming back and read them.

His ambiguous sex, passivity in the face of being taken advantage of, turning to authorities for help and finding that they are not much help— all are elements in common with his dream reports of the year before.

The subjects of our experiment who fell into this pattern of response to REM loss may have been deprived of most of their REM sleep, but they did not appear to be nearly as greatly deprived of their dreams. What is more, they did not need to recoup the REM time that was lost when they next slept without interruption.

There were other response patterns: some subjects, who reported very little dreamlike activity when awakened, showed definite increases in REM time above their previous levels as soon as deprivation was stopped. For such people dreaming appears to be intimately tied to the physiology of the REM state: deprivation of one entails loss of the other as well. These "REM-bound" dreamers we called the *rebounders* because they compensated for loss of REM not by an immediate intensification of dreaming, but by experiencing a delayed increase in REM sleep.

Thus even though these subjects were in many ways very much alike —all bright, young medical students—they exhibited different ways of adapting to the loss of small amounts of REM time. Furthermore, between nights in the lab the student subjects' waking behavior varied according to how they reacted to the experiment. Each subject was provided with a daytime companion to make sure he did not nap or fall asleep in class and who was instructed to keep notes on his charge's behavior. When they arrived at the lab each night subjects were asked if they noticed any differences in their routines—in eating or smoking habits, mood, or ability to sustain attention. Those who had reported some dreaming when we awakened them in the sleep lab appeared to get through days as if nothing much out of the ordinary had happened, except for some heightening of activity levels. They reported they could get more done during the day than usual. Subjects who were not reporting dreams at REM onset, on the other hand, found it hard to get through the days. A typical companion's report was: "I don't know whether he was asleep in class or not. He was sitting with his head propped up and a rather glassy look in his eyes." One of these subjects said of his own experience: "Well, I tried to watch what was going on, but other pictures kept coming between me and the lecturer's face."

In such cases it is as if a portion of the REM state were breaking through into the waking state after a build-up of REM loss was reached. The element that becomes disassociated from sleep is the visual imagery. If this can occur during the day when there is high informational context, we might expect it to be even more likely at night in the lab, when the subject's sleep is interrupted and he is being kept awake to prevent the REM state. This has been tested (Fiss, Klein, & Bokert, 1965; Starker, 1970) by asking subjects to view a rather vague picture and make up a story about it (the Thematic Apperception Test) (Murray, 1938). The stories these subjects created when awakened at the onset of REM were more fanciful, bizarre, and emotion-laden than those they related when awakened during NREM sleep or when they were given the same test during the day. The shift from NREM sleep into the REM state is apparently accompanied by a shift to a more imagistic, emotional, nonlogical thought style which tends to persist for a while even if the sleep itself is interrupted, providing we do not hamper its expression. What if, instead of allowing the REM-deprived person to indulge in a fantasy, we engage his attention in the opposite kind of task? Will his need to dream increase?

We tested this (Cartwright & Monroe, 1968) in another study of REM-deprived student subjects by asking them what was going through their minds and encouraging them to elaborate on any internally generated fantasy they could produce at each awakening; on another night, we required them to repeat a series of numbers read aloud to them by the experimenter. Both tasks involve loss of a half night of REM sleep, but beyond that there are three major differences between them: (1) In the fantasy-elaboration task the subject may engage in a right-brain imaging experience; in the other, this is prevented. (2) The number-repetition task requires the subject to attend to external stimuli, whereas the fantasy comes from within himself. (3) To perform the repetition task well, the numbers must be processed in a correct linear sequence, a left-brain function.

What we found was further evidence that dreams can be replaced without REM. When subjects performed the number tasks instead of being allowed REM sleep for half the night, their amount of REM sleep in the second half of the night was greater than their normal amount. After performing the fantasy task for half the night, only normal amounts of REM sleep occurred. The better each task was performed, the greater the effect on the following REM. The more numbers a subject recalled correctly and the faster he responded, the more his REM time increased afterward. Conversely, the richer the subject's fantasy report, the less REM sleep followed. The amount of REM recouped after REM loss thus seems to depend on the amount of dreaming or analogous activity that takes place in its absence.

## Personality and Response to REM Loss

Our finding that people vary in their tolerance for REM loss, in how quickly the substitution for dreaming occurs, led us to undertake still another REM-deprivation study. This time we hoped to learn something more about these differences, with the help of a battery of psychological tests (Cartwright & Ratzel, 1972). Who are the "substitutors" who report a good deal of dreaming at REM onset? They turned out to be quite different personalities from those who had a delayed REM rebound effect. Although the two groups were equal in overall intelligence, they had a different pattern of strengths and weaknesses in performing various types of intellectual tasks. "Rebounders" did poorly on tests requiring imagination. In fact, they did more poorly on all tests which tapped right-hemisphere (nonverbal) functions, scoring lowest on the ability to organize a group of pictures into a sequence telling a story or joke and to copy patterns using colored blocks and higher on vocabulary and math tests. The substitutors showed no such discrepancy in their ability to solve the different types of problems, performing equally well on both verbal-math and spatial-picture tests.

The Rorschach Inkblot personality tests confirmed these differences. The rebounders proved to be more "extroverted," more controlled by the demands of external situations than by their own inner feelings and impulses. Their waking personality patterns were highly reality-oriented but empty of fantasy. The substitutors were more equally responsive to both their inner feelings and the demands of external reality. After the loss of REM time, this group showed no change on these tests. Presumably, the substitution of dreamlike fantasy at night enabled them to weather the REM loss without a change in waking functioning. But this was not true for the rebounders. Those who did not substitute for dreaming found themselves in quite a different psychological state after their three nights of "sleep surgery." Surprisingly, after REM prevention the tests of these externally oriented, fantasy-poor, highly verbal, and reality-bound young men all revealed more evenly balanced personalities: their ability to see relationships among people increased, they got more in touch with their inner resources for fantasy, and in general they were responsive to both inner and outer stimuli where feelings and fantasy were used to enrich reality. In fact, after REM loss, they looked more like the subjects in the first group.

We thus appear to need from our dreams a period of time when the brain is active, or perhaps when the right hemisphere is more active, when the flow of mental experience is of a different kind than it is during our predominantly left-brain activity of waking life. What happens to us when we have REM sleep loss appears to depend on how we normally distribute our attention during our total twenty-four-hour cycle and how we generally organize our relations between our internal and external affairs. Those whose waking time is dominated by verbal-logical activity, who are fantasy-poor, faithful to reality, who constantly scan the environment for information to tell them who they are and what they should do, might be expected to be more dependent on their REM time at night to reestablish touch with themselves. Those who shuttle back and forth between their inside and outside experience by day, checking out their interactions with reality against their inner feelings, might be expected to have less immediate effect from dream time loss.

Is there a third sleep-pattern type—those who are unbalanced in the other direction, who have too little reality contact by day, who perhaps dream too much?

So far, our strategy of examining dream function through REM reduction has helped isolate two personality types: those whose organization of waking experience is dependent on the input of external information with little contribution from their internal stimuli; and those whose conscious experience is a product of both internal and external information. What about those whose attention during waking life is occupied strongly by fantasy, whose behavior is minimally responsive to outer reality and more to the demands from within? Under these circumstances, is there less nighttime dreaming or dreaming which has less intensity? This question leads us into the investigation of those who either "dream" more than usual or who have an unusual distribution of dreamlike activity. These are the waking hallucinators and those who deliberately withdraw attention from the external world (the meditators, for example). A look at these may give us more understanding of dream function.

Five

# EXPLORING DREAM FUNCTION
## II. The Effects of Dreaming Too Much
## or at the Wrong Time

In attempting to discover the role of dreams in our lives by examining the effect of their loss, we found that removing the REM sleep state does not necessarily prevent dreaming. People vary in their tolerance for REM loss. When this type of sleep is suppressed, the various elements of this state which ordinarily occur together begin to split off from each other and distribute themselves differently in waking and in sleep. For example, the penile erection which normally accompanies dreaming occurs at the usual ninety-minute intervals whether REM sleep is present or not (Fisher, Gross, & Byrne, 1965). Although the rapid eye movements themselves do not occur in the other sleep stages, NREM dreaming appears to become more frequent and bizarre. Some dreamlike thought can occur in the waking state as well.

Whether dreaming is reinstituted quickly or slowly when REM is removed, and whether this is distributed throughout NREM sleep, intrudes in waking, or is saved up for longer-than-normal REM periods on recovery nights, sooner or later dreams reassert themselves to occupy their fair share of our mental prime time. In other words, some homeostatic function seems to be involved in maintaining a stable proportion of dream activity in each twenty-four hour period. What is still unclear is whether it is attention to inner and outer information that must be kept in balance, or the types of mental activities associated with the right- and left-brain hemispheres, or conscious and unconscious material.

One approach to sorting out these possibilities is to examine the other extreme—when dreaming is extended beyond normal limits. Do we rebalance our economy by dreaming less in our next night's sleep—and will our waking functioning be affected as a consequence? What happens to the sleep of those who pay excessive attention to inner experience during waking time? These include people who hallucinate during a psychiatric illness or after taking certain drugs and others who voluntarily withdraw attention from the external world for periods of meditation. In all of these cases waking time may have more than usual amounts of dreamlike properties.

### Long and Short Sleepers

Not all instances of excessive dreaming occur in waking time. Some adults habitually sleep nine or more hours. The sleep patterns of these "long sleepers" differ markedly from those of the "short sleeper" who sleeps less than six out of every twenty-four-hour cycle (Hartmann, Baekeland, & Zwilling, 1972; Webb & Agnew, 1970). While these two groups have equal amounts of delta sleep, long sleepers have twice as much REM time as do short sleepers (Hartmann et al., 1972). One study conducted by Hartmann, which compared these two groups, reported that they differ also in behavior and lifestyle and on their psychological testing scores: long sleepers tend to be nervous worriers, socially introverted, with less energy, aggressive drive, and ambition. Further, they hold a positive attitude toward sleep, considering it important, while short sleepers consider sleep a waste of time and would like to be able to do away with it. Long sleepers easily recall their dreams, which are more primitive than those of the short sleeper. Long sleepers' dream life includes more sex and aggression, but their waking life contains less. In general, this study found that adults who chronically sleep and dream more than usual function less well during waking hours, experiencing too little direct action and real gratification. These differences were not confirmed on another sample by Webb and Agnew, except for the short sleepers having more waking vigor.

Besides the chronic "sleepaholics," there are those who sleep and dream more only on occasion. These latter include women during the week before menses. At this time they have higher amounts of REM than is usual, especially if they are prone to experiencing premenstrual tension, irritability, and depression (Hartmann, 1966). Perhaps when we all are nervous, irritable, and depressed we need to dream more to deal with this material. This may be a vicious cycle, because when we have more REM time, we wake up more irritable and depressed. Certainly, we know that when a person ordinarily sleeps seven-and-a-half hours and then extends this to nine or ten hours — say, on a Sunday morning — he usually wakes up listless, worn out, depressed. Everyone who has done this recognizes the kind of sleep hangover which takes three or four hours to shake off. The reason for this is that the first half of the night supplies all the delta sleep we need (See Fig. 1). Sleeping longer than usual thus extends the period during which there is a high proportion of REM sleep. Since REM sleep is a state of heightened activity equivalent to an equal period of jogging, it is no wonder that after excessive amounts of REM we wake up "more tired than when we went to bed." Even if REM sleep is good for something, it still seems to have an optimum point after which it gets to be too much of a good thing. Exceeding this limit seems to lower waking mood and drive level, while deprivation of REM has the reverse effect, that of increasing drive level and, for the depressed, mood level as well. There seems little doubt, then, that REM is related to the regulation of energy levels and mood, and that we need just enough to feel contented and energized.

What about dreaming? Must it take place during REM? If there is a psychological need for a balance between paying attention to the external information that bombards us during waking and dealing with the internal information from our inner selves, is it just a matter of convenience in our action-oriented society that we divide these tasks into day and night?

### The Relation of REM and Dream Functions

The relation of the two components of REM — the psychological experience of the dream and the neurophysiological state of activated sleep — can be one of a number of kinds.

1. The dream component may have no function at all. It may be strictly incidental. When the brain is highly activated during sleep the visual cortex may be producing random images which have no inherent meaning and no logic guiding their selection or ordering. In other words (so this argument goes), dreams do not express or illustrate psychological processes at all. Their apparent storyline is something we arbitrarily add on, much as we "add" meaning to inkblots in the Rorschach test. The function of dreaming from this viewpoint may be physiological, to keep the sensory system or the coordination of the eyes (Berger, 1969) in good working order.

Since we cannot see another person's "dream movie" as it unfolds, some researchers have sought evidence that dreams have psychological meaning by monitoring their "soundtracks." If subjects could be trained to sleep-talk during REM and report their dreams as they were dreaming them, it was reasoned, this might give us a direct pipeline to their plots. Several attempts have been made to train people in this procedure (Bertini, Gregolini & Vitali, 1972; Hauri, 1972), but it is difficult because of the profound relaxation of the muscles of the chin and throat throughout the REM state—almost as if we were specifically designed to keep our mouths shut about our dreams.

2. A second way in which REM sleep and dreaming may be related is that each has functions independent of the other but which usually occur at the same time because REM provides the right kind of conditions for dreaming. Two of these conditions mentioned before appear to be the partial shutdown of the sensory input system and the presence of a highly activated brain state. When the sensory system is not receptive to external data yet the brain state is active, internally generated data can occupy attention. If we can then duplicate these conditions in a state other than sleep, dreamlike activity should be experienced. These conditions are approximated during waking states in some psychoses, under the influence of some hallucinogenic drugs, in some meditation states, and under sensory-deprivation conditions like solitary confinement. In all of these, dreamlike experiences take place without sleep.

3. A third possibility is that a major function of the physiological state of REM sleep is to insure that dreaming takes place regularly. If this is true, the presence of dreams apart from REM might result in less REM. Jouvet and his colleagues are quoted by Dement (1969), who has also shown that when cats are given a drug (PCPA) which changes the chemistry of the brain and induces complete insomnia, they appear to experience waking hallucinations. They jump and stare at blank walls as if they were "seeing things." When they are allowed to recover and sleep normally again, they show no REM time increase or rebound. Similar reports have been made of humans who hallucinate during waking (Zarcone, Gulevitch, Pivik, & Dement, 1968; Gillin, Jacobs, Fram, Williams, & Snyder, 1972). Schizophrenic patients who actively hallucinate during waking hours, for example, do not show an increase in REM sleep after they have been REM-deprived. Unfortunately, it is hard to tell to what extent either the hallucinations of psychotic humans or of cats are equivalent to dreams. Psychotic hallucinations are more often auditory than visual, and they seem to lack the storylike quality typical of a dream. Cats, of course, won't tell.

The problem of getting good reports is central to this work, as we are completely dependent on them in determining what the person is experiencing. Part of the problem of getting good dream reports is that whereas dreams are largely products of right-brain activity experienced in nonverbal, imagistic language, we inquire about them in verbal terms, which requires the dreamer to translate his experience into left-brain (verbal) terms. Adding to the difficulty is the fact that the electrical activity of the fibers connecting these two hemispheres, the corpus callosum, is greatly reduced during REM (Berlucchi, 1965). During dreaming, then, it is possible that the left brain knows very little about what is going on in the right. In the ideal experimental situation, the subject's left brain would be awake and reporting while the right brain was engaged in dreaming.

### Drug-induced Hallucinations

Experiments with hallucinogenic drugs make it possible to approximate this ideal situation. Hallucinogens induce experiences during wakefulness which share many of the qualities of dreams. Drug-induced hallucinations, like dreams, are largely visual, but may also involve other senses. As in dreaming, there is a temporary suspension of reality testing, so that people experiencing such fantasies believe them to be real while they last. Drug-induced hallucinations also appear to be related to subjects' current concerns, and also like dreams they are very rapidly forgotten. Subjects given minimal doses of hallucinogens might thus be in that ideal experimental state, straddling the inner and outer worlds, able both to experience visual hallucinations and to report on them verbally.

In the early 1960s, before the public outcry at the street trade in and abuse of these agents, legitimate research on the effects of hallucinogens was still possible. It was then that we decided to use this method in a study to discover the effect of waking "dreams" on the amount of nighttime REM sleep. A group of normal, intelligent, highly articulate university students volunteered to take an experimental drug for one day and to sleep in the laboratory for four nights of monitored sleep, three nights to establish their normal REM percent and to collect their dreams and one night after the drug to look at the effects on REM percent. None knew the identity of the drug they would take or its expected effects. Most supposed it would be a sedative, since they knew the study concerned sleep. They were told that they might experience some pupillary dilation and perceptual effects. A few asked if LSD were to be the drug involved, and were assured that it was not.

The purposes of the study were really two: to discover (1) if hallucinations artificially induced during a waking daytime period are similar to those naturally occurring in nighttime dreams, and (2) if so, whether undergoing this experience during waking time would affect the total amount of REM time in the night's sleep that follows. If dreaming serves some normal psychological function, will a day of waking hallucinatory activity "use up" some of the need for REM on the following night?

The subjects were injected with 3.5 milligrams of Ditran (piperidyl benzilate) (Abood & Biel, 1962; Cartwright, 1966), a very mild dose of this drug. Prior to this study, the same drug had been safely used for activating chronically depressed patients at levels of 20 to 60 milligrams. The students spent the next five or more hours describing their experiences as they occurred. I stayed with each of them throughout the time the drug was active, and kept them at their task of reporting and prevented them from drifting off to sleep. External stimuli were kept at a minimum so that they could concentrate on their internally produced perceptions, although this proved difficult. One of the first effects from the drug was an intensification of some colors. Skin tones—their own hands, for example—appeared as bright orange or red, which fascinated them. Those who were feeling kindly toward me asked where I had gotten the great sunburn, but those who were not thought I was now showing my true colors as a red devil.

Before attempting to answer the question "Are waking hallucinations similar to normal dreams?" it is necessary first to indicate the nature of the state the subjects were in while under the influence of the drug. Were they really awake? According to outward indications, yes. Their eyes were open and they usually sat up and talked; but their EEG records looked very different from either normal waking or sleeping records: they can best be described as a mixture of the two. The brain wave records show that the subjects were in a highly aroused state, more rapid than the fast activity of REM, with a good deal of muscle tension and signs of both Stage 2 and Stage 3 sleep. The eyes were abnormally active, with many rapid eye movements of very high amplitude. The answer must be that they were in an "altered state of consciousness" (Itil, 1970).

What was the nature of their experience during this time? Did their experiences have the characteristics of dreams? They certainly "saw things" and believed in their reality. Their thinking was very regressive, loose, and, like dreams, full of symbolic condensations. Unfortunately, there was also a severe loss of immediate memory. Before they could reply to a question, they forgot what it was that they had been asked. This, together with the looseness of the associations, meant that their verbal flow was disconnected, meandering, and hard to follow. Although their attention was sometimes split, so that one part of their minds observed and commented on the other, this was often anything but helpful. When I tried to elicit an answer to a question by calling one student by name, he replied: "Don't bother him now; he's asleep."

## Test Responses

To attempt to measure the effects of the drug on the mental activity of the subjects psychological tests were administered both several days before and one hour after injection of the drug. Testing subjects once they had taken the drug was a long, difficult process because of their great difficulty maintaining attention. They behaved as though they were the helpless targets of a heavy barrage of stimuli both from their inner world and from the outside. They complained that they were at the mercy of all these things coming at them, each demanding equal time. They often answered questions that I did not ask but that they claimed to have clearly heard. Just as often, they did not hear me when I did speak because they were attending to something else that seemed more important, like counting the holes in the acoustic tile. One subject, who had the mildest response to the drug and thought he had been given a placebo, described this loss of control of attention as he experienced it: "Objects in the room seem more obvious. They catch my attention more. I was in a placid mood before the injection, whereas now I feel I have to pay attention to all the details and common objects, like the window." For some, this need to attend to everything amounted to a kind of paranoid suspiciousness, a reading of big meanings into small events which ordinarily would have been ignored or merely treated as background.

This lack of control of attention and loss of patterning of perception into figure and ground meant that subjects could not concentrate long enough to give accurate answers to test questions. Their answers to the intelligence test questions were peppered with errors showing the kind of loose thinking that was going on. These have a rambling, personal quality and were more concrete than the highly abstract answers they had given under the normal predrug circumstances:

> (*Question: If you were lost in the forest in the daytime, how would you go about finding your way out?*)
>
> If this is a picnic, [I'd] have someone go across the street, get in touch with [a] regular doctor. He would advise not to give injections.

In this response, the subject associates the question with his own problem of feeling lost due to the drug effects, and he wishes for help from a "regular" doctor, not the one who gave this injection. This response is rather like the thinking involved in a wish-fulfillment dream.

(*Question: What does this saying mean: "Strike while the iron is hot"?*)

Means take the opportunities given to you and do not procrastinate between two girls.

The subject gives a correct answer, but this starts a chain of personal associations with a present emotional concern. Sometimes this loosening of associations actually took the form of an hallucination:

(*Question: Why should we keep away from bad company?*)

Oh, pardon me. [*Subject is aware he has been day "dreaming" and reports this as his answer:*] I was still working where I worked and a friend of mine came in and told me that he was making $1.75 for doing nothing and here was I making only $1.50.

The question about "bad company" reminds him of the "unfair (bad) company" he works for, and this stimulates a minidream. Sometimes the creation of a hallucination in response to a question was quite vivid:

(*Question: What does this saying mean: "Shallow brooks are noisy"?*)

Perhaps the guy doesn't feel acceptable. Possibly he has a bad tooth. Does it hurt much? [*This was addressed to an imaginary patient by the subject, who was a dental student.*]

Test errors due to the intrusion of other stimuli into the subject's attention were numerous. Sometimes these were from external sources, sometimes internal, and often both.

(*Question: In what way are a dog and a lion alike?*)

One's tall and the other short. I decided to work backwards from the vagus nerve. Is the color in that hallway a very, very bright yellow?

(*In what way are a table and a chair alike?*)

Mostly wooden. Hold out your hand like this. Just a little tremor there.

(*Who are you talking to?*)

One of the medical students.

Reading these curious responses, one might think that these students were deliberately trying to be funny. Quite the contrary. They struggled hard to perform well, to cut through an information overload which they had difficulty channeling into a succinct reply. Their EEG records during these sessions confirm that there was simultaneous activation of too many different systems which ordinarily operate separately.

While the drug was still active, the subjects were also asked to repeat a figure-drawing test they had taken previously, requiring them to draw two complete figures, one a male and one female. The theory is that the test taker projects into this task his own body image, that these drawings thus reflect his feelings about himself. The drawings subjects made under drug influence were, predictably, very different from the previous ones. They show the subjects' concepts of their bodies to be much more primitive, less well-developed and mature. The figures are uniformly smaller, simpler in form and detail. Often they have regressed in age from adults to children, or in form to monsters, and appear undressed rather than dressed. (See Figure 4.)

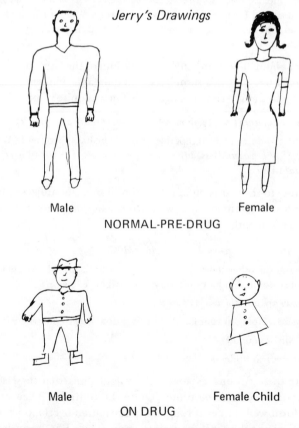

FIGURE 4. Examples of figure drawings under normal and hallucinogenic drug conditions

## Don's Drawings

Male

Female

NORMAL-PRE-DRUG

Dead Person of
Indeterminate Sex

Male Child and
Female Child

ON DRUG

FIGURE 4. (Continued)

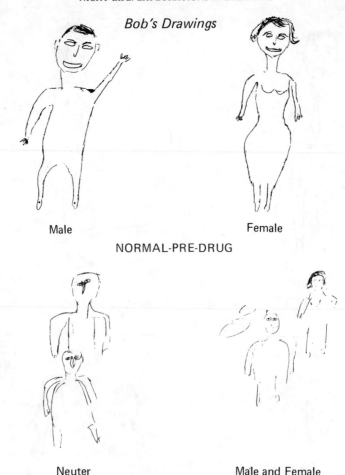

*Bob's Drawings*

Male                    Female

NORMAL-PRE-DRUG

Neuter              Male and Female

ON DRUG

FIGURE 4. (Continued)

One of the participants in this experiment was Don, whose dreams were reported in Chapter 2. Like his first lab dream (see Chapter 2), Don's first drawing during his drug-active period is of a dead person. Also characteristically, he said it was of "indeterminate sex." Only with urging could I get him to draw a male and female figure. Bob, who was prone to nightmares of monsters (see Chapter 6), made five attempts before his drug picture resembled anything human.

Altogether, the test responses show that during the drug-active period the nature of the information being received, the ability to select and con-

### Carl's Drawings

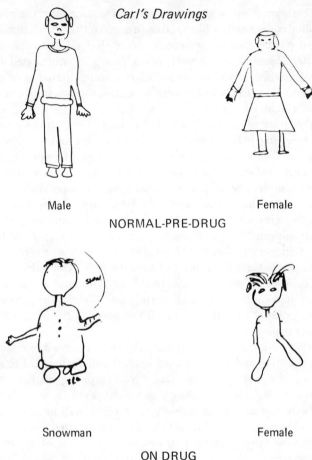

Male

Female

**NORMAL-PRE-DRUG**

Snowman

Female

**ON DRUG**

FIGURE 4. (Continued)

trol its flow, and its interpretation were all abnormal. While the drug effect was strongest, contact between innner and outer worlds was broken for a time. Although "awake," the subjects were unaware of where they were and unresponsive to my attempts to call them back to "reality."

### Varieties of Hallucinations

The subjects' hallucinatory behavior at the peak of the drug effect can best be described as a one-way telephone conversation. They talked to people not physically present and appeared to be engaged in activities they did not report: "Let's get it up on dry land"; "Who's looking after the patients?" These episodes were rather like waking dreams in that their attention was all focused on the internal perceptual world. Judging from the subjects' speech, they appeared to be actively participating in hallucinated dramas. Not only were they responding to stimuli that were internal in origin, but they lost the ability to control attention, to shift focus, and to test this internal material for its validity.

At the more moderate levels of the drug effect, subjects were apparently receiving both internal and external information, often at the same time and sometimes alternately. In one type of response, subjects reacted to external stimuli but gave them unrealistic, personal interpretations. For example, one subject perceived a lamp as a person looking over my shoulder who he greeted and called by name. Many times, I was mistaken for someone else—girl friend, wife, roommate, or professor of some other subject: "Are you going to wash your hair tonight?" "What's for dinner?" "Can you stay over until Monday?" "Do you have any questions on the cardiac cycle since it's going to be on the test?" One subject reached over and took off my shoe. All explained later, with some embarrassment, whom they had confused me with at the time. Clearly, the subjects were perceiving external stimuli in terms of the needs of their internal world without any reality testing at the time.

In other instances, new, imaginary objects were added to reality. One subject sat holding an imaginary book in one hand, turning the pages with the other, as if studying. Another said: "Nice carpeting you have on these walls" while feeling the floor, which was uncarpeted (as were the walls). One sat watching something intently on a blank wall and, when asked what he was watching, said: "A nucleus. Pretty good sized tissue around it. Cells with something phagocytizing away in the middle of it." Jerry, the farmboy whose dreams were reported in Chapter 2, was also a wall watcher. He watched: "An old man in a hog pen bending over to pick up a corn cob and the hog butts him in the rear end." He enjoyed this "movie" a good deal and laughed out loud. Another subject reached out to the wall saying: "Alice in Wonderland falling down a hole." Subjects added these internally generated dream images to their external world without any apparent recognition that the sources were different.

In another type of effect, subjects' perception alternated back and forth between external reality and internal fantasy, the storylike fantasies taking place during lapses of attention to reality. When external contact was regained, these fantasies were tested and recognized as unreal as they were being reported. They usually involved a short drama taking place in some other locale than the lab. For example, Don said suddenly: "Going fishing without a fishing pole?" When I asked him what was up, he replied:

> I was dreaming. We went and picked everybody up, three friends and me, and we found we had no money so we walked along Fifty-first Street. Didn't you see? They were all getting out of their cars with fishing poles and going to sit on the rocks. It was crazy. Apparently, it didn't translate well.

## Similarities of Dreams and Hallucinations

Are these experiences dreams? One way to answer that question is to compare them in terms of their themes and symbolic language to the dreams reported by the same subjects from their normal REM sleep periods. To do this, we asked a psychologist unfamiliar with the subjects to try to match the subjects' dream reports with reports of their drug-experiment experiences. He was able to correctly pair up more than half of the records.

The subjects' drug-induced fantasies and their dreams, in other words, appear to have been drawn from the same source material; the symbols they used to express these were also similar. Sometimes this was quite clear. Jerry, for example, spent most of his drug hallucination time trying to do a job too big for him, just as he did in his dreams. In the drug experiment he relived his adolescent experiences with his father. He kept looking for spare parts for a car which was constantly falling apart; doors, handles, fanbelts, and tires kept falling off despite his efforts. Don, on the other hand, who had grown up on the South Side of Chicago and been threatened there, hallucinated that he was wandering around the South Side trying to be nice to people, but to no avail. Another subject had had a single constant theme in all his dreams on his night in the lab. He was always flying F-105 jets over Vietnam, bombing villages and being chased and hit by missiles. During his drug day, he hallucinated weapons and war images. At one point, he pointed to a "design" on the floor and said: "You ought to use that kind of a design on your fatigues. It would be good camouflage." At other times, out of context, he said: "Oh, those marching hours; north, south"; "This is a scout expedition of the German army. An American version of the Alamo"; "I thought I saw a whole chain of machine guns right there in a row"; "That looks like a Thompson gun, a fifty-round magazine in it"; "See that? A missile there. Can you reach over and get it? I thought I saw a missile. It's a prayerbook, really." Although these hallucinations were scattered over a five-hour period and constituted only one of his themes during the drug session, it was obviously an important one for him.

## Effects on REM

Even if the subjects' daytime, drug-induced hallucinations resemble their dreams, can they serve as substitutes for dreams? After a day of this activity while awake, will there be a reduction in the amount of REM in the sleep that follows? The average predrug proportion of REM sleep for this group was 24 percent. On the night following the drug session, this was reduced to 13 percent. However, we cannot say with certainty that this was caused by the abundance of dreamlike experiences during the prior waking time, for the subjects' sleep recordings indicated that the drug was still active that night and was disrupting the normal EEG patterns. That is, the low proportion of REM may have been strictly a drug effect. Even so, this study was valuable in showing that "the stuff that dreams are made on" can occupy attention during the waking state—and will tend to do so when conditions are right. As in REM, the brain state during the drug-active period is a highly activated one. Both states are also characterized by a disruption of the regular processing of external sensory information and a lack of ability to control or focus attention. When this happens, one's attention is free to be occupied by interior mental activity, by images and thoughts immune to reality testing.

Do drug-induced hallucinations represent a kind of mental activity that serves some purpose? The fact that such images can be made to surface during waking is not in itself convincing evidence that they have an independent status or function. To establish if dreaming, whether by day or night, has a logic, we must first discover if it is a language with a grammar; and to discover whether it has a "psychologic," we must understand not only what is being said, but to what purpose.

Approaching the question of dream function in this way means we must examine dreams in context. Can we trace how a dream is formed? Can we induce a person to dream of a particular subject by putting him in a particular mental state before sleep? If so, we may be able to learn how this experience is represented in dream language. By carefully manipulating presleep conditions, we may be able to see their effects on dreams. If subjects are deprived of water, will they gratify the need by a wish-fulfillment dream of drinking? Or, will they express the need in dreams of deserts and the hot sun? If the dream images in fact relate to immediately preceding waking experiences, in either way this would support the notion that dreaming is part of an ongoing thought process. If their relationship, on the other hand, were of some other nature, it would seem that dreaming is a more enigmatic affair. Any systematic relation we find between the experimental stimulus and the dreams that follow provides an opportunity to learn something about the laws governing relations between our daytime and nighttime though processes.

# Six

# EXPLORING DREAM FUNCTION
## III. Learning How Dreams Are Formed

The evidence we have so far examined seems to support Jung's conception that we experience a continuous flow of mental activity from which dreams emerge when the time is right. This dream-stream can be thought of rather as the bass of a stereo system: we are usually unaware of it while it is over-ridden by the treble of the day. When we tune out or turn down this higher channel, we clearly hear the other which has been playing all the time. But out of all that flow, what determines the particular dream that emerges?

### Why *That* Dream *That* Night?

Some dream images are so clearly related to a preceding waking event that they are delightfully apparent. One night, during the worst of Chicago's famous three-foot snowstorm, when movement about the city was very difficult and worrisome, one of our subjects participating in a REM-deprivation study made it to the lab with difficulty for his night of awakenings. At the onset of his first REM period of the night, when he was called on the intercom and asked, "What was going through your mind at the moment I called you?" he replied, "I was shoveling green snow out of the driveway." He then laughed and added in an excited voice: "Hey, that must mean spring is coming. The snow has turned green!" Here, in this simple dream, the theme represents a continuity with the real presleep experience of coping with the snow, but the image which expresses it involves a distortion. This serves an additional purpose beyond representing reality; it reflects the wish that it be different.

Before we feel too clever at decoding this image, we must ask: Could we have predicted it? Given our present state of knowledge our answer must be that, of all the many things that occurred to this subject before sleep, there is not way for us to predict which will be the one selected for a dream theme or how it will be represented. The green snow was a simple symbol. Others are much more tortuous to trace and may have their roots far in the past, and yet be elicited in response to a particular event occurring prior to sleep.

### Tracing the Origin of a Nightmare

One of the subjects in the hallucinogenic drug study, Bob, whose figure drawings appear in Chapter 5, reported only one dream on the night when his normal dreams were collected. The dream upset him so much that he had trouble getting back to sleep and was unable to recall any other dreams for the rest of that night. No doubt the dream's major symbol is heavy with meaning for him, but when he was asked about it in the morning he had no clue to understanding it. As he reported the dream that night, he was breathing irregularly and exhibiting other signs of panic.

I believe I was in a lab, biology, with about ten other guys and the instructor. There was a big tank of water and it had this monstrous fish in there. It was—I don't know how to describe it—the big thing was circular and had a mouth on the bottom and didn't have any eyes. It was supposed to be some sort of primitive octopus with no tentacles. Some crazy thing. And he was making a demonstration that this thing could eat without having eyes to see. It didn't look at its food, it just knew when the food was there. He threw something in the tank, and this thing just kind of gobbled it up, and that's all I remember. The instructor was one of the guys from the microbiology department, of all places. I remember his name was Dr. Vicher, V-I-C-H-E-R. [pronounced "Visher"]. Maybe I could say a couple more words about this fish or whatever it was. It was in a big tank and there was no lid on top of this tank and I guess it was about three-quarters full of water. Anyway, this thing was not exactly round, more oval, sort of egg-shaped. It was flat on the bottom but on the circumference it was sort of egg-shaped and the mouth was toward the pointier end and it sort of pulsated, you know, got bigger and smaller and that was about it. I was surprised that this thing could . . .

when you threw meat in the tank it just glommed it up and it was gone and it went munching away.

In the morning, he added these remarks:

The big thing was maybe three feet long, two feet across, and a foot thick at the bottom with the mouth on the bottom like a shark's mouth. It shrank up, sort of contracted a little bit, and then swelled up all of a sudden and just leaped right at this food and just engulfed it. I remember the instructor was Vicher. I remember his voice. He was saying, I don't know, it's so crazy, that you could put this big thing into a little teeny bottle and keep it there for twenty years or something like that and it would live in the little bottle like a genie, I guess. (*Question: Can you relate this dream to anything that has happened to you lately or that you can think of in real life?*) Good grief! I don't think so.

The fish symbol was primitive, frightening, and disgusting to him. The expanding and contracting, the idea of staying bottled up for twenty years and suddenly swelling as it satisfies its hunger—these sounded very phallic in structure and sexual in function. It also has very feminine components; the egg shape and mouth on the bottom. Yet none of this explains or satisfies the questions Why *this* dream at *this* time? Why a fish? and Why Dr. Vicher? Vicher sounded like a combination of Vicious and Fisher, and this reminded me of an anecdote that Bob had told earlier in the evening while he was taking his intelligence test. To the test question "If you were lost in the forest in the daytime, how would you go about finding your way out?" he replied, "You know, I really was once lost in a forest. My father took me fishing and he was so interested in the fish that he lost me. I didn't find my way out. I cried." Bob, though very bright, made no connection between the dream name Vicher and Father = Fisher + Vicious Loser of Little Boys.

Bob was given the same test item again two weeks later while he was under the effects of the drug. This time he made no reference to the childhood incident. He talked instead about his present life and that he was glad to be living away from home because he "fought like crazy with my brothers," all six of whom slept in the same room. When I asked "Who was boss in your house when you were growing up?" he replied: "Father, I guess. He's the Big Tuna. Got that name from Tony Accardo." Here is the association Father = Big Fish = Vicious Gangster. Tony Accardo was a noted Chicago underworld figure.

Bob continued to talk about his father and brothers: "One wanted to be a detective [but] there is more money in setting up stills and letting the federal men catch you." Stills reminded me of the tank in the dream. I asked then if he remembered getting lost in the woods on the fishing trip with his father, and he said, "My father is a fanatic about fishing. He heard about this lake in the woods with really big fish in it and nothing would do but I had to go with him. Whatever he says goes, so I went and he lost me."

The dream symbol was probably created many years ago, but was stimulated to appear in the first REM period by his recalling the incident of being lost as an eight-year-old while he was talking with me shortly before bedtime. This was a very anxiety-laden memory. It was followed by another anxiety-arousing situation: sleeping in the lab. This experience, involving as it does being public about private matters, coupled with the fact that several young men are prepared for sleeping at the same time, may have reminded him of his home sleeping arrangement with his many brothers. This may be what is represented in the dream as the "ten other guys" in the biology lab. The public sleeping situation may also have brought to mind either a real or fantasized memory of watching the Big Fish(erman) and his mother make love at a time when this seemed an incomprehensible, frightening, disgusting event.

Why this symbol is chosen for the night is not immediately clear. Perhaps the fact that I, a female older than he, prepared him for bed aroused old oedipal feelings. What is important to note for our present purpose is that both dream images, the obvious green snow and the less obvious primitive fish, can be traced to events which induced some anxiety during the evenings preceding the dreams. This fact raised our hopes that it might be possible to understand dreams and their function by controlling the presleep situation. If a group of subjects were all exposed to the same stimulus, the source of dream images could be interpreted more easily, and the subjects' use of this common material in fashioning different dream plots could be explored with more confidence.

### Choosing a Target for Dream Construction

How should a stimulus be chosen to yield optimal chances that it will be incorporated into the subjects' dreams? Should we intensify some basic need like thirst (Bokert, 1968), or satiate one like exercise (Hauri, 1966)? Should we use an emotion-arousing stimulus like a violent film, or something neutral (Foulkes & Rechtschaffen, 1964)? Should we employ something as generally arousing as a group therapy session, or as specific as the preoperative night for surgery patients (Breger, Hunter, & Lane, 1971)? The effects on dreams of all of these have been studied. What we have learned from all this is that controlling what people dream is a mighty complicated business. In one study (Bokert, 1968), inducing thirst by serving a spicy meal before sleep led subjects to dream about water and thirst; but in another (Dement & Wolpert, 1958), subjects deprived of fluids for twenty-four hours before a night of dream collections reported no thirst themes in their dreams. What if, instead of depriving subjects, we "overloaded" them before sleep? One study, which required subjects to perform six hours of physical exercise before sleep, found less physical activity than usual in their dreams (Hauri, 1966). In another study, subjects were satiated perceptually by requiring them to wear rose-colored glasses for two weeks. Their dreams did not contain less color or even the complementary color, but were, in fact, rosier (Tauber, Roffwarg, & Herman, 1968).

Generally, some confusion in experimental results seems to be due to a failure to establish just how the subject relates to what is being provided or withheld. How important is it to the subject, and how does he cope with its presence or absence? Is he a water freak or a camel who can go for long periods without touching a drop? Also important is what the whole experimental situation means to the subject. Is he a person anxious to please the experimenters and to give us what he thinks we want or someone out to beat the system? Does it make a difference? If it does, and if both types are represented in a group of subjects, we may wind up finding out nothing if the two response styles cancel each other out.

We felt that a movie might be a useful presleep stimulus for studying dream formation if it were carefully chosen for high intrinsic interest value. If we then selected subjects with very different orientations toward the film's subject matter, we might get better insight into how waking experience is translated into dream images.

Two previous studies of this kind had been done. In one (Foulkes & Rechtschaffen, 1964), two episodes from a favorite TV series were shown. One night the subjects viewed a very violent episode before bedtime and on another night a humorous episode. The subjects seemed to ignore the content of the shows completely and to dream their own personal dreams. The only effect was a similarity between the level of excitement in the dreams and the shows. After the violent episode, dream reports were more lively. The authors concluded that the subjects were too jaded with TV to take these shows very seriously, that they could watch this kind of material without it having enough real impact to involve them personally. In another study (Witkin & Lewis, 1967), stronger stuff was used. Four films were used, one each night. One film pictured childbirth aided by a vacuum extractor, a rather bloody business. Another showed a tribal initiation ceremony for young boys in which the skin of the penis is split with a sharp stone. A third film, which was taken in a primate-study lab, showed a mother monkey dragging around and eating her dead baby. These were alternated with a very bland movie, a travelogue. As might be expected, the strong films had greater effect on dream content than did the travelogue. After viewing the birth and initiation-rite movies subjects' dreams had more sexual content than was the case with the monkey movie; but the experimenters made no attempt to relate the dreams to the specific presleep state of each dreamer.

### The Effects of a Stag Movie

Following this lead, we selected a "stag" movie as our presleep stimulus. We showed the film to two groups of male subjects, one heterosexual (Cartwright, Bernick, Borowitz, & Kling, 1969) and the other homosexual (Kling, Borowitz, & Cartwright, 1972), anticipating that the two groups would respond to this experience with different sorts of dreams. This film was made up of two ten-minute segments. The first is set in an English brothel in the eighteenth century. A young man is shown selecting a girl and taking her to a bedroom where they drink some wine, help each other undress for bed, and get into the traditional position for coitus. The second segment is set in the present time in a hotel room. A bride and groom enter, have drinks, undress during much foreplay, and then engage in fellatio, cunnilingus, and several varieties of intercourse.

Perhaps the young men of today are too jaded by exposure to pornography to respond to this kind of stimulation as well. The entire project staff previewed the film and responded to it strongly. One of the male staff members, who claimed he had an ample and satisfactory sex life, reported that two weeks after seeing the movie he dreamed a complete rerun. Realizing that it might take some time for this material to come to the surface in obvious ways, all REM periods were interrupted for dream reports for four nights following the subjects' exposure to this stimulation. These dreams were then compared to dreams collected on a night before the film was shown.

Interpreting the results requires that we first discuss a little theoretical background. If the dream stream contains personal emotional associations to the current waking experience, and if this information processing is an efficient system, it should continue in sleep, processing only those parts of experience that have not reached some closure. Under this assumption, either the central elements (of stimuli during wakefulness) which attracted most attention or those on the margin of awareness could become grist for the dream mill, if not completed. (*Completed* or *closure* in this sense means that tension reduction has taken place through either action or thought: a decision had been reached, a need gratified, or information assimilated and categorized.)

We expected to find the theme of the movie influencing only the dreams of those subjects who did not complete their response to it during waking. We reasoned that if the film aroused a given subject physically and psychologically and that in addition he (1) had no chance to reduce this tension in action or fantasy before sleep, (2) had multiple associations to this material because it was a high-interest area, and (3) was motivated to cooperate with the experimenter, then his dreams would include sexual images and themes. If, however, a subject was not aroused or interested, or motivated not to report sexual material, we expected his dreams to be tamer or to feature other themes.

Both the heterosexual and the homosexual subjects wore a penile strain gauge which showed they were, in fact, sexually aroused by the movie. Nine of the ten "straight" subjects and eight of the ten "gay" subjects had moderate to full erections while watching it. By this evidence, they were aroused and not satiated before sleep. Each interpreted the stimulus in ways appropriate for them. The heterosexuals reported right after seeing the film that they were turned on by the female, the homosexuals by the male. In their daily lives both groups were active sexually and were interested in this subject matter, a fact established by depth interviews beforehand. Where they differed markedly was in the degree to which they defined the laboratory situation as one in which it was appropriate to share these interests with the experimenters. The heterosexuals were medical students at the university hospital where the study was being conducted and where the experimenters were faculty members. These subjects reported at the end of the study that they felt a good deal of pressure to control their sexual fantasies in our presence in order to convince us that they could be "responsible doctors"—doctors not likely to get aroused and "act out" in the hospital setting. Their dreams were full of examples of their concealing their sexual impulses and interests. Quite the opposite was true for the homosexual group. They were all activists, members of a national group's chapter at a neighboring university. Their motivation in offering themselves for this study was one of public service. They saw this as an opportunity to educate us about homosexuality and through us to influence the straight world not to be so hard on them. Their motivation to be open was strongly apparent in their dreams.

## The Dreams of the Medical Students

After viewing the movie, none of the heterosexual medical students reported any explicitly sexual dream. Their dream reports tell us that their interest in sex is, like the experimenters', purely scientific and that when they are exposed to situations in the hospital that are potentially sexual, they can be trusted to stay in their proper professional role.

I was dreaming about Florida, walking along with a male friend of mine. We were with some graduate students and visiting a *professor** down there *who was analyzing all sorts of wild data.* . . . Then I asked the professor if he still needed anyone to go out and collect sea urchins for him [that] they needed for *fertilization studies.* The next thing we were walking and kind of continuing the conversation about going out for sea urchins and I was telling him what a pleasant experience this was.

I was *walking through* a patient's room in order to get to another one and she had just returned from the operating room and had on one of those *little short robes.* She was indignant that I had gone through her room and made some remark about it not being a thoroughfare. (*Like a prostitute's room, but he makes a point that he does* not *stay.*)

I had just walked into a room where a young man and a young woman were changing the diaper on a new baby. I don't know whether I was supposed to be a doctor, but it was obviously a hospital. She wasn't, you know, *in bed* or anything. She was standing up. Neither one were in hospital robes, but they did have a new kid and *I seemed very interested in the kid,* you know, the way it looked and the fact that it was healthy and so forth. (*Looking at sexual organs for a medical purpose.*)

## The Dreams of the Gay Students

In contrast, after viewing the film the homosexual subjects had explicitly sexual dreams with obvious enjoyment.

I was making love. It's hard to remember the details. I remember I was right on top of . . .

I was back in that room, or that sort of garden. Hefner was there. Hefner and I had been talking philosophy. We wandered back into that restricted courtyard and went through the door there. And there was this man sort of fiddling around with this young girl and the other young girl looking on. I thought, "He's so jaded this is what he has to do to amuse himself." And

*[Italics added for emphasis here and in other dream reports throughout the chapter.]

there are two guys who eventually started to give each other blow jobs and I, I joined in, finally.

I was talking to some people. . . . There was a beautiful blond boy who was sitting with a very fat girl . . . and the girl asked me which one I would rather go to bed with and I said, "Probably your friend," and she sort of smiled. . . . All of a sudden the boy was in my arms. The girl didn't seem to mind at all and he was kissing me very violently, no, passionately, and sort of arranging himself in various positions. Finally, he turned over on his back and I started to lick his back very sensuously. I did that for a while and he really seemed to like it.

### THE DREAMS OF BOTH GROUPS INVOLVING AUTHORITY FIGURES

The two groups showed a real difference in their motivation to be open with us. Of course, there was the direct expression of the enjoyment of sex in the gay group and its denial under the professional guise among the heterosexuals. But additional evidence came from dreams in which the subject is in a potentially sexual situation in the presence of an authority figure. The heterosexual subjects' dreams show their fear of being "caught in the act" and concern with looking good under these circumstances. When an authority is present in the dreams of the homosexual subjects, they take an active teaching role and explain to them how it really is to be gay.

The first of these dreams was reported by a medical student on the night before seeing the movie; the second is a postfilm dream.

Music. I think it was violins or something. It was in color. This time the music was in the living room of our apartment and I had my girlfriend there. I had undressed her and we were *about to make love* when there was a knock on the door and it turns out that it was *her parents, of all people,* and they acted like nothing was wrong. Like I don't know how she did it, but she *got dressed almost instantly.* The reason why they came wasn't very clear. . . .

I had been to see my old girl friend, the one from New York. She was living at a dorm and we often had a habit of staying too late. Well, in this case, I overdid it and the ladies closed the door and for some reason, instead of asking to get out I went with her upstairs and stayed in the bathroom of the little cubicle she was living in with another girl. The other girl didn't know that I was there, so apparently I just slept in there *standing up* all night long. The next morning there was an *inspection of the room and I was caught.* The girl I was going with was gone and I had no explanation of how I got there so I was in kind of a tough spot. *The lady* who was doing the inspection was very nice about it. In fact, she wasn't the least surprised when she opened the door and found me standing there. (*Although caught, by an authority he is innocent.*)

The next three dreams were all from homosexual subjects, after seeing the film.

It was a really dramatic scene in which some doctor—well, it's like I had already finished this experiment and this *lady doctor* was terribly scandalized by the fact that I was a homosexual, and she said, "If I had only known what you were for," and I said, "That's not true and that's not the approach you should take and, uh, *you don't understand what it's all about.*" And I was very gentle and kind and all that and she sort of broke down and started crying. And I just explained the way things were. Just pointing up the fact that some people make money the center of their lives, and some make taking care of their children the center of their lives. And in the end, a lot of them make this some sort of monomania. And with homosexuals, ofttimes the center of their lives can just be sex. But at the same time, they might be intelligent as far as money matters are concerned and so on and so forth, but they can never, never forget [*very dramatically*], uh, that they are homosexual and that sort of broke both of us up.

It was a sort of *press conference* and we were talking about the fact that *Gay Liberation was trying to do something good* for the community with regard to a certain person and we weren't getting any support. In fact, members of the community were trying to destroy the organization. I was standing in front of a large machine which reminded me a lot of those newspaper racks they have in libraries where the newspapers are on poles that hang like flags. Anyway, we were in front of a rack and we were illustrating various points of the press conference by pulling out the rack and there were pictures on there. This was after there had been some bloodshed and a lot of trouble and people were saying, "Oh, what a shame," you know, "that we didn't see these events sooner so that we could have prevented them." . . .

A bathroom has some *male enlightenments*. There was this *old lady* going through some things of her father who had died and she was looking for a book called *Male Enlightenments*. The room looked like the master bedroom of my mother and stepfather. She was cute but real old and was trying to get this book *Male Enlightenments* in order to learn some sex techniques. It was funny because she was too old for that sort of thing. I liked her and *helped her find some things she was looking for.*

## Do Dreams Preserve the Self?

One principle that emerges from the study just described is that dreams are apparently formed in response not only to needs aroused before sleep, but also to the emotional meaning to the subject of the whole situation. These two may be compatible with one another or in conflict. In either case, the dream response is such as to preserve and protect the waking self. Both groups were sexually aroused by the film, but in the context of the lab this was seen as appropriate by the gay subjects and inappropriate by the medical students. This difference is clearly reflected in the dream themes the two groups formed and the roles they assigned themselves in their dream dramas. The most common self-character role in the medical students' dreams was not Lover, but Student or Doctor; the most common in the homosexuals' dreams was Friend (to another male) or Homosexual. Rarely did the gay subjects assign themselves an occupational identity in their dreams, and equally rarely did the medical students cast themselves in a sexual role.

It would be interesting to try to equalize the situations for the two groups. If the medical students saw the same movie in a lab remote from their hospital, with lab personnel who had no connection with their institution, this would be a better match for the gay subjects' experience. Then we could test whether the lack of explicit sexual dream activity was particular to the specific setting or more generally characteristic of these subjects.

Aside from the difference in the meaning of the situation for the two groups, there was another difficulty with the way this study was designed. The stimulus was too complex. A twenty-minute film has too much in it. It becomes almost impossible to try to trace all the objects, activities, and feelings expressed from the film into the dreams. It would be better to provide a simpler situation, preferably a single event, which could be counted as being either present or absent in the dreams that follow. Despite these difficulties, the study gave us a clear hypothesis concerning dream function that we considered worth testing: dreams are formed to reaffirm the self-concept.

### The Wish-to-Be-Different Study

With this in mind, we looked for a stimulus that subjects would define as their own rather than as one imposed upon them—one that represented something personally relevant to each of them, some unresolved tension or uncompleted task which could be brought into the focus of their attention just before sleep. To find such a stimulus, we asked subjects to describe themselves using a list of adjectives. Each subject was given a deck of seventy cards, one adjective printed on each card (Block, 1961; Cartwright,

1974b), and asked to arrange them on a scale by placing words they considered most descriptive of themselves at one end and words least descriptive at the other. This they did twice just before getting into bed. The first time, they laid out the cards to describe their present view of themselves, and the second time to describe themselves as they would most like to be. We then identified for each subject one trait which he rated as most like him now but least like his ideal for himself; this word became his presleep stimulus. As he was falling asleep, he was asked to repeat that word over and over to himself, and to wish to be more like his ideal. If, for example, the word describing the quality with most discrepancy was *jealous*, the subject was to say: "I wish I were not so jealous. I wish I were not so jealous." In this way, each subject had a personally highly relevant presleep stimulus —the wish to change that quality which he least admired in himself. The dreams that followed were then collected. The presleep stimulus trait showed up significantly more often as a quality of the dream characters than other adjectives of equal importance to him but not used as presleep stimuli. How the dreams were formed around this target word confirmed the results from our erotic movie study. Subjects do *not* dream that they have reformed. Instead, the dreams show that they are enjoying themselves just the way they are; the present self is reaffirmed. One subject, whose instructions were to wish she were not so sarcastic, had two dreams in which she expressed herself very sarcastically to authority figures with a good deal of satisfaction:

> I was walking through a big department store and I had just come back from lunch. I was talking to this cop who must have had ten dollars worth of food for lunch and he said, "What does your mother think of all of this food?" and I said, "I don't know, she's not here with me. . . ." And the cop was—I wish I could swear—he was just a real mean guy, a real wise guy. I told him he ate like a pig. Except that I caught myself because you don't call a cop a pig, of course, but he was really eating a lot. . . . I was kinda *having a good time telling the cop what an animal he was.*

> I was walking home . . . and all of a sudden I saw the whole sidewalk was covered with my bedspread and all of these people were walking on my bedspread, and all of a sudden this schoolteacher came out who was my neighbor, and I said, "Look, lady, that's kinda taking liberties on my bedspread. I ought to have you fired." And she said, "Well, I've got more brains than you," or something, and I called her a bitch or something, but she had ripped my bedspread. . . . This lady—*I really wasn't very diplomatic with her*, like I was immediately *very mean* to her—and she really snapped back and then I said something like, "Well, *at least my mother's not an old biddy like you.*"

### Dreams as Protectors
### of the Self under Attack

Dreams restore the waking self, as presently defined, particularly when this is under attack. When the medical students felt their professional identity threatened, their dreams presented them as proper students and doctors. The homosexuals, who felt it was their sexual identity which opened them to threat, had dreams which expressed and defended themselves as good people in their sexual role. When the waking self-image of the students in the adjective study was directly threatened by our instructions that they wish to be different, their dreams denied that they felt any discomfort with their present self. In both studies, the dreams provided emotional support for the dreamer's self-identity. Both the stag movie, a highly explicit visual stimulus, and the adjective, a rather abstract verbal self-stimulation, were followed by dream images and story-lines whose common function was a reaffirmation of the salient features of the self.

This, then, appears to be one primary function of dreaming: "knitting up the raveled sleeve of care" by restating who we are and justifying our waking behavior when it is under attack. At least in healthy individuals, dreams have this goal and provide this efficient coping process. Clearly, this is not so in all dreams. It does not fit those reported in Chapter 2, which we interpreted as a response to the general anxiety aroused by the presleep laboratory situation. Jerry's dreams dealt with the threat to his competency as a male after the exposure to a more competent older woman. For Don, the threat appeared to be to his ability to control his fears regarding homosexuality. Both were real current problems, unknown to the experimenter. Neither set of dreams can be said to have restored the dreamer's self-image.

For Don and Jerry, however, the lab situation was quite different in this respect. No explicit, focused attack was made on their soft spots. The experimenters were supportive but noninterfering allies in their dream voyages. They were free to dream their dreams. No attempt was made to either predict or control them. The problems revealed in their dreams were probably not ones in the direct focus of their awareness before sleep, but those on the periphery of their attention. In contrast, the subjects in the movie and adjective studies were in a more highly structured situation. They were quite aware of the intended dream topic for that night. Their attention was deliberately focused, in both cases, on an area of some uneasiness to them.

### Dreams as Rehearsal

When the situation before sleep is nonspecific but accompanied by general anxiety, the dreams that follow are progressively clearer statements of a particular personal problem along with some suggested solutions. This appears to be a second dream function: dreaming brings to mind the data relevant for exploring a personal emotional problem when this has not received enough direct waking attention or has not yet reached closure. If this is true, then this clarification may be useful work from which we ought to derive some benefit, although there is still some question whether this can occur if the dreams are not interpreted or even recalled. Frontal attacks on a person's areas of vulnerability appear to provoke a dream defense of the self, while exacerbating a chronic problem by using indirect reminders brings about a further exploration of the problem's emotional ramifications and possible solutions. In the one case, the function of dreaming seems to be ego restoration; in the other, the function may be one of preparation.

Like other need-related behaviors, dreaming may well serve multiple purposes. We eat not only to maintain life, but also to grow, for gustatory pleasure, to reduce anxiety, to be sociable, and for various combinations of these and other motives. To understand the purpose served by any one act of eating, we need to know a good deal about the present state of the person as a whole, including his recent and related past. He may be eating a handful of peanuts not because he is hungry, but because he is bored with the TV show he is watching and eating offers a change of sensory input. Dreaming, too, may sometimes serve as comic relief or a change from the boredom of NREM sleep. The uses of dreaming may turn out to be as many and complicated as the uses of waking thought and to depend on the most urgent present need or needs.

If dreaming performs the useful functions of the sort suggested by these studies, it should have some testable effect on how we subsequently view problems. For example, are we closer to the solution of a problem after having "slept on it" than if we had spent an equal time awake? Perhaps not in some quantitative way, but dreaming may supply new ways of thinking about problems which can then influence our waking choices.

# Seven

# THE PROBLEM-SOLVING FUNCTION OF DREAMING

## Are We Smarter in Our Dreams than When Awake?

The idea that dreams may be a resource for creative thinking and problem solving is one that has recurred frequently throughout history. If the mind asleep operates without the usual demands of faithfulness to external reality as we know it and to the rules of logic, yet continues to deal with our unresolved current concerns, is it not likely that some of the images generated to express these concerns contain fresh ideas worthy of being retained and translated into action? Many examples testify that this is not just wishful thinking. In fact, some of the finest products of the arts and sciences have been attributed by their creators to dream inspiration.

### *Dream Solutions*

Robert Louis Stevenson (1925) spoke of his "little people" who "share my financial worries and have an eye on the bank book." When these worries became pressing, it was the little people who supplied help through dream images. "They share plainly in [my] training, they learned like [me] to build the scheme of a considerable story in progressive order, only I think they have more talent." Stevenson credited this kind of collaboration between his waking and dreaming thought with the writing of *The Strange*

*Case of Dr. Jekyll and Mr. Hyde.* The theme, of the double nature of man, was one he had been struggling to write about for some time. A sudden financial crisis made it imperative that he produce a saleable story quickly. After two days of fruitless waking effort, he dreamed the crucial scenes: Hyde taking the potion in the presence of his pursuers and undergoing the change back to Jekyll, and the central idea of a voluntary change becoming involuntary. The rest was waking construction and plain hard work.

It is said that the breakthrough idea for the design of the special needle that made the sewing machine possible was also the product of a dream. In this case, too, many days of waking effort and an exhaustion of logical ideas was followed by a dream solution. The insight came in the form of an image of a harpoon in which the thread passes through an eye at the sharpened end, rather than at the other end as in a hand-sewing needle. In both cases, the dream occurred at a time when there was a heightened need to resolve a problem and followed a long period of concentrated thought which had eliminated some of the obvious possibilities. Such circumstances seem to set us up for a night of problem-focused dreaming — and probably also for a night of lighter, more restless sleep, which would allow better dream recall. Do creative dream-answers come only to very creative people and then only under these unusual circumstances? Or is there a good deal of this productive activity more commonly going on everywhere, but just not being remembered and understood? And if the latter, are these solutions completely lost, or do they nevertheless affect our waking behavior, guiding us without our awareness?

Even a brief acquaintance with modern research on sleep and dreaming reveals that our night life is indeed a very busy time. The concept of sleep as a period in which we are peacefully at rest, recouping from the activity of the day past, and storing resources for the struggles that come with the light of morning has given way to quite a different view. Sleep is a time of continuous mental activity. The shop is never shut down for the night. It may be that the machinery is kept going primarily to insure that it is in good working order when it is again needed, but it is also possible that the night shift turns out some useful products which could enrich our lives, or at least save us some time in thinking through our problems.

Dreams appear to be formed in response to emotions aroused by our prior waking experience; dreams follow where these feelings take us. Stimulation from some current personal concern activates related memories, fantasies, and associated images and makes them available for dream production.

Before sleeping in the laboratory one night, one student was sharing with me a pressing personal dilemma: Should she give up her graduate program to stay home and be a "good" wife to her new husband, or should she attempt to finish her Ph.D. first? She went to sleep with this question unresolved. That night, she dreamed that she was standing in the kitchen of her apartment holding a textbook. As she looked at it, the book turned into a potholder. On examining it more carefully, she discovered a hole in it and decided it "wouldn't work very well because I'd burn my hand." In this one image she stated her feeling that it would be a mistake for her to trade in the book to be a cook. Did this represent a continuation of her waking thought, reaching the same conclusion she would have reached if she had stayed awake? Or did the dream represent an emotional response to this problem, different from her "logical" waking conclusion? She did not, in fact, make her waking decision in the direction of the dream. Instead, she took a leave of absence for two years, during which time she had a baby, planning afterward to return to school. Her real-life solution was based neither solely on the conscious demands which dominated during the day nor on the inner feelings which spoke in her dream, but on a compromise which integrated these two.

Some dreams are responses to waking problems, and dream images are assembled according to a different set of rules than is waking thinking —that much seems clear. That these two types of thought might well lead to different conclusions is also apparent to anyone who examines many dream reports. That dreams may contain good ideas, if not routinely at least on some occasions, does not seem farfetched. Now, is it also possible that dream thoughts carry over and affect our waking thought without our knowledge? If "sleeping on it" changes the way a problem appears the next day, it should be possible to test for this effect, to see if a "dream residue" becomes incorporated into the next day's thinking. This is another way to approach the question of dream function. It proposes that as waking experience affects dreams, so dreams in turn affect waking behavior and thought.

### Memory Studies

There is some evidence that supports this idea. It appears that the work of processing and storing new information into long-term memory continues during sleep and that for some kinds of learning this process may actually be more efficient during sleep than while awake. This evidence has been accumulating over the past fifty years in studies comparing the ability to recall newly or partially learned material after a period of waking time with the ability to recall such material after an equal period of sleep. More recently, these studies have tested not only the general effects of sleep on memory, but the ability to remember after a period of sleep including some REM as compared with a period in which only NREM sleep occurred. In this way, the effects of REM on memory can be separated from a more general sleep effect. Another way this is explored is to test people for their ability to remember both after REM deprivation and after sleep with an equal number of interruptions made during NREM stages. Although there are contradictions among the findings, the evidence now appears to be slightly in favor of the conclusion that there is better memory after some dreaming has taken place than there is after an equal interval of waking time or of NREM sleep. This appears to be particularly true if the material to be learned is personally relevant and emotion-arousing.

Why should REM sleep be involved in fixing new learning of this kind in long-term memory? When early studies were conducted in the 1920s and 1930s (Jenkins & Dallenbach, 1924; Van Ormer, 1932), researchers had no knowledge of the different sleep stages. These experimenters thought of sleep only as a quiet time during which there is less opportunity for outside distractions to interfere with newly learned information. Of course, the concept of sleep as peaceful is more accurate for NREM than it is for REM.

The first of these studies cited above showed that newly learned material is rapidly forgotten during the first two hours, whether the period is one of sleep or of time awake. After that, though, things are different. If we test for recall after three, four, or five hours of sleep, the same amount will be retained as was remembered after the first two hours of sleep; there will be no further loss. If subjects are awake, on the other hand, they will forget progressively more from hour to hour after the first two hours. Perhaps the occurrence of the first REM period during the first two hours of sleep somehow serves to hold new material in an association network, preventing further memory loss until awakening.

There are two factors that seem to affect memory following REM sleep: the relative personal importance of the material being learned and the freedom from interruption of the sleep interval (Empson & Clarke, 1970). Presumably, if the material being learned is rich in personal meaning, it lends itself to multiple associations in the dream periods, which aids recall in the morning. Any interruption of sleep which shifts attention outward and introduces extraneous stimulation seems to disrupt this process (Muzio, Roffwarg, Anders, & Muzio, 1972). In general, if we want to recall new material, it is best to be alert, in an active brain state with focused attention and little interference from competing stimuli. During waking hours we experience an active brain state and the ability to focus attention, but outside interference is often high. During NREM sleep, all of these factors are low, but REM may provide the ideal conditions, since while cortical arousal is high interference from the outside world is low. The more personally relevant the information, the higher its arousal value and so the better the recall (Kliensmith & Kaplan, 1963).

## DO WE RECALL MORE?

Students sometimes ask whether staying awake all night studying for an exam is worth it or whether they are better off getting a good night's sleep. Does REM sleep aid memory when the material is not personally relevant but we know we will need to recall it in the morning? This question was studied by one of our students (Barker, 1972).

Subjects in this study slept in the laboratory for five hours. They were then awakened and gotten out of bed at about 4:30 A.M. and told they were to learn something before going back to sleep. They were shown slides of line drawings of common objects; a cat, bed, star, and pair of shoes, for example. After two run-throughs of these slides, they were asked to write down all of the objects they could remember. They then went back to sleep for another two hours. Since the last two hours of sleep is the period when there is the greatest concentration of REM time, we could test the possible benefits to memory of an interval of dreaming. A few of these student-subjects were not able to pick up the sleep cycle where they left off after being awake for the learning period. These subjects had only NREM sleep during their last two hours. Most of those who had some REM sleep either showed no memory loss or actually remembered more of the slides in the morning than they had before they went back to sleep. All of those who had only NREM sleep after viewing the slides recalled less in the morning. To check whether the same subjects recalled differently while awake they were tested for their ability to recall similar material without any sleep in between. All showed some loss over two hours (see Figure 5). These findings support the idea that there is a memory benefit in the morning from previous REM activity.

## DO WE RECALL DIFFERENT MATERIAL?

Post-REM memory for new information may be better, but is it different? Does dreaming change the nature of what was put into the system? When information is recalled in the morning, has dreaming made an ac-

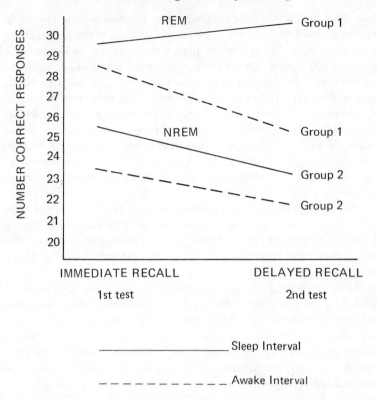

FIGURE 5. Number of correct responses following waking and sleep intervals

tive contribution to it? Specifically, if the association networks of dreaming are different in kind from those of waking, do these affect the recalled material? If the same material goes through two programs operating on different principles, it might be expected to lead to a different output.

We wanted to test this proposition with material which would have real personal meaning. To insure this, we chose the adjective test we used before in Chapter 6's wish-to-be-different study (Cartwright, Lloyd, Butters, Weiner, McCarthy, & Hancock, 1975; Block, 1961). Words such as *ambitious, bossy, cruel,* and *dull* were printed on a deck of cards, one adjective to a card. Again the subjects described themselves by sorting these onto a board with compartments. Those they considered most descriptive of themselves they placed on the side labeled "Most Like Me," those least descriptive on the side labeled "Least Like Me." The remaining cards were distributed in order of the degree to which the subjects felt the adjectives were "like" or "unlike" them. Once they finished sorting the cards to describe themselves, they were given a second deck of the same cards and sorted them again to describe the person they would most like to be. This procedure allows us to rate the words for personal relevance. After the board was removed, the subjects were asked, unexpectedly, to write down as many of the words as they could remember. They then went to sleep for a night of interrupted sleep. One group was awakened at each REM onset to prevent as much dreaming as possible. The second group was awakened toward the end of each REM period to preserve most of their REM sleep while equalizing for interruptions. As soon as they were awakened in the morning, the subjects were asked again to list all the adjectives they could remember.

Both groups showed some memory loss over the course of the night in terms of total number of words remembered. This was much more pronounced for the REM-deprived group. Two subjects who had been allowed most of their REM time recalled more words in the morning than they had the previous night.

More interesting, though, was the difference in the kind of material recalled by the two groups. Some subjects recalled words in the morning that they had not remembered the night before. Four of these "new" words were unique to the dream group: *ambitious, cautious, competitive,* and *reasonable.* As a group, the words have an action-oriented ring to them of engagement with external life, social control, and realistic thought. Subjects who were REM-deprived recalled only two new words which were unique to them, *selfish* and *self-indulgent,* which are quite different in connotation. Is this accidental, or is there some other evidence for a true difference between morning recall when REM dreaming has occurred and when it has not? Aside from their new words and despite their generally poorer level of morning recall, the REM-deprived group as a whole remembered three words more often than did those in the REM sleep group: *imaginative, introspective,* and *unconventional.* All have to do with response to inner stimuli. This is like an effect we reported in an earlier study. In that study, after three nights of REM deprivation, the subjects were found to be more internally oriented and better in touch with themselves (see Chapter 4).

Although it is always risky to generalize from experimental results based on very small numbers of cases until they have been confirmed by further studies, the trends are interesting and consistent. Sleep with dreaming appears to be followed by improved recall of material appropriate to the active, striving, waking life to come. The kind of words better recalled after normal amounts of REM were those relating to interaction with others and to achievement-oriented behaviors. In contrast, a night of sleep deprived of some dreaming was followed by an increase in the recall of egocentric and inner-life words. It is tempting to conclude that those who have dreamed have attended to the business of their inner life. They have had time for their selfish, introspective, imaginative, unconventional thoughts in this period. Their active and interpersonal needs have been held in abeyance while they slept, and these have increased in strength and come to impress themselves on attention as this is turned outward on awakening. It is the REM-deprived subjects' needs for inner experience that have been frustrated. They are not ready to turn their attention back to the outer world. These findings support the hypothesis that there is a need for a balance of attention. In waking, the proportion is more toward outer stimuli, in dreaming toward inner stimulation. When dreaming has taken place, attention is ready for the shift back to the outer world of reality, and when it has not, it remains focused on inner experience.

Since after a period of REM there is better recall of some kinds of experience, it seems that some active processing of waking experiences must be taking place during this state. What is more, this must be of a different kind than goes on in waking. We know that REM periods do not begin immediately after the onset of sleep, yet dreams associated with them contain recognizable elements of experiences from the previous day. The underground stream of associations must keep flowing. These are worked into new combinations with older material from the past and with fantasies of future expectations. During the falling-asleep period and first NREM sleep, the work of processing this uncompleted waking experience must be started. The topics which go into this dream pool seem to be those that are relevant to our current concerns. Once dreaming begins, so does the ouput from this work of assimilating and associating the new experience to the old. This leaves the decks cleared in the morning for renewed attention to outer reality interaction.

## GENERALLY SUPPORTIVE EVIDENCE

Other evidence to support that dreaming is involved in information processing, sorting, and storing is meager. What evidence there is, is largely correlational. We know, for example, that the amount of REM sleep and age are correlated (Roffwarg, Muzio, & Dement, 1966; Feinberg, 1969): infants and young children have the highest proportions of REM, the elderly the lowest. This can be interpreted as some support for the argument that REM has an information-processing function: during the ages of greatest new information acquisition, REM is highest; while it is lowest when we have the most repetition and the fewest new kinds of experience. Among a group of aphasic patients who had lost the power of speech, those who were judged by two speech therapists to be relearning their speech had higher proportions of REM sleep than those who were judged not to be recovering (Greenberg & Dewan, 1969). In another area of research, newly hatched chicks have been found to have the highest REM proportions during the critical period of imprinting—while they are "learning" to respond to the visual pattern of their mother and to follow her (Greenberg, Kelty, & Dewan, 1969). This high REM figure drops suddenly at the end of this period. In mice, too, there is an elevation of REM time during and immediately after new learning (Fishbein, Kastaniotis, & Chattman, 1974; Smith, Kitahama, Valatx, & Jouvet, 1974). Both adults and children who are severely mentally retarded show lower-than-normal REM proportions, delayed onset of the first REM period of the night, and fewer eye movements (Feinberg, 1968; Castaldo & Krynicki, 1973). Among retardates, the lower the IQ, the lower the proportion of REM (Feinberg, Braun, & Schulman, 1969; Castaldo, 1969). The implications of all this is that REM is proportional to the amount of new information that is being processed and stored, and that some organisms capable of handling less information also have less REM time.

For humans within the normal range of intelligence, there is at this time even less evidence that REM has this learning function. In one study (Zimmerman, Stoyva, & Metcalf, 1970), subjects wore glasses throughout the entire day which reversed their field of vision (either left-right or up-down). The experimenters reasoned that this should dramatically increase the amount of new visual information which would need to be learned quickly and old schemata which would have to be revised. If REM were involved in this kind of learning, this kind of experience should increase the amount of REM occurring during sleep intervals. They were right. REM time increased at the beginning of the period of adjustment. It dropped back to normal as the subjects got used to the glasses, but increased again briefly when the glasses were finally taken off and the old perceptual schemata had to be reinstated. All of this sounded promising, but a replication study failed to support it (Allen, Oswald, Lewis, & Tagney, 1972).

If REM is in fact involved in processing new information, one way to confirm this would be to monitor a few people in a sleep laboratory over a long enough period of time to show that there are variations in their REM proportion corresponding to periods of intensive new learning in their waking life. When there is more mental work to be done of the kind specific to dreaming, REM would presumably extend into overtime. This basic naturalistic study has yet to be done. Even to say "more mental work to be done of the kind specific to dreaming" sounds as if that were some known quality, and this is still premature.

### Effects on Emotional Material

If we assume, for the moment, that dream time is involved in processing new information according to a different program which organizes its emotional meaning, we may test this indirectly by examining the output of the dream work. If an emotion-arousing problem is introduced before sleep and carried forward in dreaming, it should result in a different kind of orientation to the problem in the morning than if it is worked on only during a waking period. Will the solution be, if not a creative breakthrough, at least of a different emotional quality? Does our access to REM time, and all the wealth of past associations and imaginings that this brings, help us cope better in our waking lives? Are problems solved differently when put on a back burner before coming to a conclusion during a busy day than when an equal period of time is spent in sleep that includes REM? In testing this idea, it is important to choose the kind of problem for which dreaming may be expected to make a difference.

One study that exposed subjects to ego-threatening material before sleeping found that they had better recall in the morning if dreaming occurred than if there was only NREM sleep (Grieser, Greenberg, & Harrison, 1972). In another study (Greenberg, Pillard, & Pearlman, 1972), subjects were shown a stress-producing movie and then allowed to sleep. Those who dreamed showed less stress reaction when they were shown the film a second time than did those who were REM-deprived. The latter subjects showed as strong a stress response the second time as the first. Both of these studies suggest that dreaming may serve to defuse emotion-arousing material. Something about assimilating such material into its emotional context of ideas and feelings, during a period when other demands do not distract our attention, appears to be helpful to our waking ability to cope. Perhaps this is the basis for the creative ideas which sometimes occur in dreams and are recalled. REM sleep seems to provide the opportunity, while we are protected from the need to take action, to explore a wider range of relevant associations without the inhibition of logic or the fear of ridicule.

## Problem Solving

To test whether dreaming changes our view of problems the next day—
and if so, how—we gave a group of students pairs of equally difficult problems to do under two conditions (Cartwright, 1974a). In one case, there
was a waking interval between the time they began working on a problem
and the time they finished it; for the other problem, they had a sleep-
with-REM period in between. The problems they were asked to solve were
of three different types: crossword puzzles, a word-association test (Remote
Associates Test) (Mednick & Mednick, 1967), and story completions.
These were chosen to vary in content from being impersonal and intellectual to more personal and emotional. It was predicted that the more emotionally involving the material, the more likely it would be that dreaming
would influence the solution. Dreaming was not expected to increase the
number of right answers for the crossword puzzles, since there is no room
for creativity in finding these answers. Performance on the word-
association test requires more flexibility. In this test a word must be supplied that links three disparate words into a group; for example, *base*,
*dance*, *snow*, _____. This item must be completed with the answer *ball*.
Solving these requires ignoring common meaning associations and finding
less frequently used ones. Since dreaming also associates elements in un-
common ways, it might possibly help in this task. However, it was the third
type of problem which was specifically designed as the test for dream influence. This required the subjects to write endings to stories which posed
an emotional conflict problem. The subject was shown a picture from the
Thematic Apperception Test (TAT) (Murray, 1938) and told this was an
illustration for a story. He was then given a copy of an incomplete story
and asked to finish it. This task was expected to come close to testing
whether dreaming continues waking work on uncompleted emotional problems. The payoff comes when we analyze the postsleep story endings to
see whether they show any systematic differences from stories completed
after a waking interval.

Each time they were given a problem, subjects were told they had ten
minutes to work on it. After this time was up, they were told that they
would have another chance to finish it later. When the time in between the
two work periods was spent awake, the students were allowed to go about
their usual business, reporting back to the lab three-and-a-half hours later
for another ten-minute work period. For the trials with sleep in between,
only the last half of the night was used. On those nights, subjects went to

sleep in the lab at their usual time. After the first half of the night, they were awakened and given the first trial on a problem. They then went back to sleep till morning. The second ten-minute trial to finish the problem came when we got them up at about 7:00 A.M., also three-and-a-half hours later.

The findings were clear. There was no difference in crossword puzzles results whether the subjects had been sleeping or awake in between. The number of new items they could fill in on the second trial was the same in each case. This was also true of the word-association items. There was a decided difference in the story completions. After being awake, most subjects gave stories a happy ending: the hero solved the problem in a way that gratified him, even if it were at the expense of others. After a dreaming period, the story endings were less successful from the hero's point of view. Sometimes the ending might imply that things did not work out well at all and the problem persisted. Two subjects, Jim and Vic, illustrate these findings. Both wrote successful endings after a waking period and failure endings after sleeping. Furthermore, this difference was *not* due to the subjects seeing one picture as gloomier than the other, since they reacted to the pictures in exactly opposite ways.

## THE PROBLEM OF BILLY

The picture that accompanied the "Billy Problem" showed a young boy staring down at a violin resting on a table. The subject was handed the picture and instructed: "Write as dramatic a story as you can to this picture. The little boy's name is Billy. It is practice time. He wants to be able to do so much more than he can now. That's his problem. Write about how he feels and how it works out. You have ten minutes."

Jim's solution to this story followed his *waking* break. The ending was scored as "*successful*":

A whole month of practice already and still nothing but a screeching violin. Billy's dejection is without comparison. The whole thing seems so hopeless. What's the good of wasting all that time—better to be out playing football—maybe at least then he could be a famous quarterback when he grows up. Eventually, though, driven by the knowledge that he must practice for at least forty-five more minutes, he takes up his violin and tries. Funny thing, after a few minutes, his music doesn't sound so bad—and it can be fun! By the end of his allotted practice time he's not ready to quit. A few years later, Billy, though not a famous violinist, is good enough to play with the school orchestra, where he is acknowledged as one of the better musicians.

Vic's solution to this story followed his *sleep* break and was rated "*failure*," since he didn't resolve the problem in his composition:

> Billy had started violin lessons since about five weeks ago. Since that time, he has had two lessons and learned two scales. His teacher is sick and he hasn't had a lesson since so all he knows is the two scales. Billy feels very glum and blue about this. He was so excited about taking lessons and now he has only had two. If Billy knew just a little more, maybe he could teach himself. Billy is very disappointed and nothing can make him feel happier.

## THE PROBLEM OF WALTER

The picture for the second problem story showed an elderly lady in profile looking out a window, while beside her a young man stands with hat in hand. This time the instructions were: "Write as dramatic a story as you can to this picture. This is Walter and his mother. They are at home. They have been arguing because he wants to live on his own. That's the problem. Write about how they feel and how they work this out. You have ten minutes."

Jim's solution was written after his three-and-a-half hour *sleep* interval. This time his solution received a *failure* rating.

> Walter's mother is a widow. She's become very dependent on Walter and uses him as a crutch. She claims she will die without him. She discourages him having girl friends and disapproves of most of his friends. Walter, in the meantime, who is in his late 20s, sees that he must break away if he is to have a life of his own. After the argument, he moves away. His mother disowns him. Within a year, Walter finds and marries a girl. Two years later they have a child. He calls his mother but she refuses to see the son who has betrayed her. Walter is somewhat bothered by this and does go on trying to see his mother. She turns down all his requests until finally he stops calling.

Vic's solution to this problem came after his *waking* break and was scored as *successful*.

> Walter is very troubled, He can't understand why his mother is so fearful of him being on his own. Sure he'll miss her good cooking and her cleaning and all the motherly duties she performs for him. But he's got to start doing these things for himself sometime. Walter thinks the time to start is now. Why can't his mother accept this? Walter's mother feels very old and useless. Walter's decision to move away makes her feel discarded and unneeded. She feels that Walter is very ungrateful. Here she spent twenty-eight years of her life caring for him and now he is leaving. She's very worried about what she is going to do with her free time. She doesn't want to vegetate in a rocker spending her time gazing out the window all day. Walter assures his mother

that just because he will be living in his own apartment that she'll still see plenty of him and his friends. He tells her that he would enjoy and appreciate having dinner with her at least three times a week. She can even clean for him and he'll bring his laundry over every Sunday. This makes Walter's mother feel considerably better. She is still worried but she is reasonably assured now that her son is not leaving her life for good.

The finding that there are more failures to work things out after a dreaming period that after a waking period does not sound very hopeful. Dreaming does not necessarily lead to "better" problem solutions. There is evidence, though, that the solutions to these emotional problems, if not better, are in fact different. The story completions were affected by dreaming, whereas problems with fixed answers were not. Dreaming changed the way the emotional problems were viewed in the morning. The subjects were better able to recognize and speculate about negative possibilities which seem to be avoided in the waking state. Since we need not take any direct action during sleep, we seem to consider and prepare for the "what if . . ." circumstances that are not so pleasant. This makes us better able to get on with the realities of the situation when we wake. This conclusion supports the findings from other studies that found threatening material is better dealt with after sleep with REM (Grieser et al., 1972) and that the reaction to previously upsetting stimuli is reduced (Greenberg et al., 1972). This study does not disconfirm the hypothesis that dreaming brings new insights to problems we have been struggling with during waking if we accept the idea that not all insights are positive. It may also be considered an insight to face the facts of irreconcilable differences. It may be that the more positive instances of creative ideas occurring in dreams — whole poems, songs, or images of perfect solutions — take more than a half-night of dreaming to work out. Dreams should be examined for a longer series of nights following a problem. Creative dreams may be more common in "creative" people, or, if they occur in all people, perhaps only when they have urgent personal problems.

The every-night dreams of the everyday person serve a number of different functions. Information sorting and storing of new experience into emotionally related categories may be one regular one. When anxiety is present, dream work seems to concentrate on retrieving and reviewing older examples of the issue, as we saw in Jerry's and Don's dreams in Chapter 2. When self-esteem is threatened, the dream material prepares a defense. What carries over to affect the next morning's view? On the basis of the study discussed above, the answer appears to be that present problems are put into perspective: "life goes on." "You can't win them all" seemed to be the message contained in some of the postdream story solutions. Such a stance may help the dreamer reorient his view of the problem so that it can be taken up more realistically the next day. If this is one function dreams perform, clearly they do not always work well. Some dreams are more upsetting than they are helpful, at least for a time, and some people do not awaken better able to cope with reality. Are the dreams of those who are psychologically disturbed different in this way? Do these people's dreams fail to do their work?

# Eight

# DREAMS AND MADNESS
## Are Hallucinations Misplaced Dreams?

Everyone who thinks seriously about dreams must sooner or later deal with their relation to psychosis, particularly schizophrenia. Is the waking hallucination of the schizophrenic a misplaced dream? Does our freedom to be mad in the safety of our beds somehow make it possible for us to be rational by day when actions have real consequences? Does the psychotic, who acts in waking life as if his fantasies were real, have less REM sleep or less bizarre dreams than the normal person? Perhaps the person who is mentally ill does not have more of these fantastic episodes than the normal. The difference may be that in the normal, dreaming is compressed into four to six episodes of REM sleep, but in the schizophrenic, this is more widely dispersed throughout all states. Would it help to restore the psychiatrically ill person to mental health if, by some manipulation, his "dreaming" could be tucked back into his sleep time? The famous psychiatrist Hughlings Jackson is often quoted as saying: "If you wish to understand madness, look to dreams" (Jackson, 1958, p. 412).

### Similarities and Differences

The first step in studying the relationship between dreams and madness must be to determine if there is any reasonable basis for the analogy. In what way are the nighttime dreams of normal persons comparable to the waking hallucinations of psychosis? It is because the similarities between these two are striking that the idea of a hydraulic model of the mind has been so attractive. In this view, a waking hallucination is a case of "dream leakage" caused by a breakdown of some control system. In both dreaming and waking hallucinations, the distinction between what is real and what is not real is lost and the most improbable events are accepted as true. In both, perceptual experiences spring from an inner source that is not recognized as such. In dreams these are more often visual in psychosis more often auditory, usually of voices. In both, feelings can run high and the experiences are strange and disturbing more often than pleasant. Also, both tend to occur in cycles of about ninety minutes.

To help determine whether these similarities are more apparent than real, the sleep of schizophrenic patients has been monitored to discover if they have less total REM time than normal people, or if there is a difference in its quality. Are there fewer eye movements, perhaps? Are the dreams themselves different? The point is to determine whether the hallucinating psychotic is suffering from a disruption of the controls between the cognitive systems of waking and sleeping which permits the same internally generated, emotionally relevant associations that operate in dreaming to be projected onto the outer world, where they are responded to as though their origin were external.

### Schizophrenic Thought

A person is usually judged to be schizophrenic if he exhibits a thought disorder. This is often described as "overinclusiveness," or the failure to exclude "irrelevant" data from thoughts or speech. It is as though the person cannot think straight. His line of reasoning is loose, idiosyncratic, and hard to follow. All of these terms refer to a difficulty with maintaining voluntary control over an external focus of attention. The schizophrenic who hallucinates seems to carry over into waking life dreamlike ways of perceiving and feeling as well as thinking. His emotions are often inappropriate, poorly socialized*, and impulsive, which is characteristic of some experimental subjects after prolonged REM deprivation (Fisher, 1965). The same connection can be seen during deprivation awakenings, when subjects are asked to respond to a picture by making up a story. The stories they create at this time are much more dreamlike, imagistic, and emotion-laden than those they create during the day. In schizophrenia, the programs which organize the dream-stream material, the inner responses

---

*Controlled by social norms of good conduct

of feelings and fantasies, are not turned off while the necessary work of relating to the external world is done. They compete with the action-oriented programs that process external information. As a result, logical processes are diverted and thoughts take off in unpredictable directions. The language in which these thoughts are conveyed is salted with puns, allusions, condensations, and symbolizations characteristic of normal dreaming.

## REM Changes in Schizophrenia

The poorly blended intermixture of the two thought styles of waking and dreaming into the waking life of hallucinating schizophrenics might lead us to expect that their night life will show some disruption of their REM sleep. On the contrary, their proportion of REM sleep does not differ from normal (Feinberg, Koresko, & Gottlieb, 1965; Koresko, Snyder, & Feinberg, 1963). However, closer inspection shows this is true only of the chronic patient who has been ill for some time and who has reached a stabilized level of the disorder. Those who are in the first phase of the disorder or who are worsening do have less-than-normal REM time in their sleep (Kupfer, Wyatt, Scott, & Snyder, 1970; Feinberg, Koresko, Gottlieb, & Wender, 1964), and in fact the REM time of recovered patients increases over normal levels (Gulevitch, Dement, & Zarcone, 1967). It seems that REM time is roughly inversely proportional to the degree of waking upset: as patients become more bizarre by day, REM time recedes from sleep; as they improve, REM sleep increases. Perhaps the mechanism that normally controls dreaming is operating again so that this type of experience again alternates with waking thought rather than intrudes into it.

## Dreams and Schizophrenia

Examining the dreams of schizophrenics confirms this picture. Dement (1955) reported that the dreams of chronic patients were notable for their blandness and sterility of content. There were usually no people in these dreams and often only a single object. This dullness has been confirmed in other studies (Arey, 1964; Cartwright, 1972). Arey suggests that when schizophrenics' night dreams begin to change and become more active and "crazy," their waking hallucinations will begin to decrease.

Studying the dreams of schizophrenics is not an easy task. One problem is that most patients of this kind are usually medicated to help control their symptoms. This affects the sleep and probably also the content of the dreams. Consequently, it is hard to tell which differences from normal are due to the illness and which to the cure. Another problem is that schizophrenia is not a simple illness but one that takes several forms. Within these, there are also different levels of severity and differing courses of the illness. We cannot generalize about the dreams of schizophrenics without considering the kind of schizophrenia involved, when in the course of the illness the dreams were collected, and how they were recorded. In addition to all of this is the problem of communication. Depending on the verbal reports of normal cooperative subjects is difficult enough. When the subject is one who is suffering from a thought disorder, which makes it difficult to understand him under the best of circumstances, the problem of the accuracy of the report becomes more serious.

Despite all these hazards, there are a few studies of the dreams of these patients. Unfortunately, none is really comparable to the others. In one (Okuma, Sunami, Fukuma, Takeo, & Motoike, 1970), the dreams of chronic hebephrenic schizophrenics who had been ill an average of ten years were compared to those of a group of younger male and female college students and to a group of psychiatrists who were of the same age as the patients. The patients had all been treated regularly with drugs, but were withdrawn from their medication for ten days before the study began. They were all experiencing waking distortions of reality, either hallucinations or delusions*. Collecting laboratory dream reports proved to involve many differences between the patients and "normals." The patients took longer to respond when awakened for a report from REM; they needed more prompting, had more failures to recall at the time, and forgot more of their dreams by the morning. Their difficulty in reorienting to reality, and in remembering dream material once they did, may be due to their problem with voluntary control of attention. The dream-reporting task asks them to do the very thing that is hardest for them: to separate their internal world from external reality on command.

The dreams that patients reported were less organized, less complex, and had more sex but less bizarreness than those of the normals. The dream feelings were more often negative; sadness, anger, fear, and anxiety occurred more often, and the dream characters were less often friends. These experimenters summarized their findings by characterizing schizophrenics' dreams as simpler, less active, and less bizarre than those of normals. Using a Freudian explanation, they suggest that these more "real" dreams are due to the failure of the patients to disguise or code their

*Mistaken ideas often of being persecuted unfairly or of being some notable figure

primitive feelings and impulses by means of dream symbols. These patients are certainly more primitive and direct in expressing their impulses when awake, and in this study these traits appear to continue in sleep. But do their bizarre hallucinations by day and "realistic" dreams by night add up to the same amount of dream experience as normals, with just a different distribution? Or do such patients experience more than a normal (total) amount of this material?

In another study (Kramer, Whitman, Baldridge, & Ornstein, 1970), the dream life of a group of male paranoid schizophrenics was explored both early in their illness, before they had been given any medication, and again after a few weeks on drugs, when their waking symptoms had begun to improve. Again, the number of dreams recalled was lower than normal, and they were less dreamlike. The lower recall rate may reflect the fact that the content was less exciting and that there was less plot development, factors that ordinarily aid dream recall. In fact, 90 percent of the dreams of these patients were rated "realistic" both before and after drugs were administered. Regarding content, before treatment began the dreams involved more strangers and more aggression, which seems reasonable for a group of paranoids.

In contrast to both these reports is a study (Carrington, 1972) of the dreams of thirty acutely ill schizophrenic women patients collected over a five-day period. This time the dreams were not collected in a lab, but were those the patients remembered without the aid of EEG-monitoring. These were compared to dreams recalled by a group of normal college girls who slept in their own dorm beds and reported their dreams when they awoke. The patients' dreams were collected not when they first woke up (because they were then "too confused and uncooperative") but later in the day. Under these circumstances, the results were just the opposite from those of the studies where the dreams were collected during the night. These patients' dreams were found to be overwhelmingly threatening, filled with mutilation imagery and morbid themes. They were more aggressive, more bizarre, and more often reflective of poor ego control than the dreams of the student control subjects. The sleeping female schizophrenics appeared to be struggling, often futilely, with massive disruptive forces (Carrington, 1972, p. 347).

How can we account for these differences? For one thing, the subjects in this last study were all women, and women have been found to be slightly better dream recallers in general. Perhaps they reported gorier dreams only because they remembered them better. Another reason why these dreams might have been more bizarre is that about two-thirds of the group were currently taking some medication, which could suppress overt symptoms during the day and make the night dreams somewhat more florid than usual. Probably most important, though, was the difference in the method by which the data were collected—having the dreams recalled later, during the day, rather than retrieved at the time by sleep interruption. Dreams recalled by normals from home sleep are also reported to be more dreamlike and bizarre and to contain more sex and aggression than those of the same people when their dreams are collected in the lab (Domhoff & Kamiya, 1964; Hall & Van de Castle, 1966; Weisz & Foulkes, 1970). Of course, the dream everyone most often recalls spontaneously is the last one of the night, which also tends to be the longest and most bizarre. This may explain why the dreams reported by these patients were more "far out" than those in the monitored sleep studies. It does not, however, account for why the dreams the patients recalled were so much more bizarre than those recalled by the normal college girl controls.

These patients were in an acute state. This means that during waking their thinking was easily disrupted by psychotic thinking. This process might be expected to color their dream recall. The dreams may well have become more florid in recollection under the influence of this thought disorder. In other words, perhaps a waking schizophrenic cannot separate him- or herself sufficiently from delusional thinking and hallucinated perceptions to give an accurate report of something that happened internally some hours ago. In short, the psychosis compounds the ordinary problem of getting a good dream report. Just as the memory of our dreams changes over time—edited, elaborated, and developed into a better story as it is worked through the medium of our waking interests and thoughts—so, too, the schizophrenic's report becomes an untrustworthy account of the original dream. If the waking hallucinations of schizophrenia are escaped dreams, dream reports given later in the day may be a conglomeration of the remembered nighttime dreams as enlivened by ongoing hallucinatory experiences.

## Schizophrenics and NREM Dreamers

There are also people who have dream experiences outside of REM time, but who are not subject to the waking intrusions of hallucinations. These are the NREM dreamers. These persons, although not psychiatrically ill, have some qualities in common with schizophrenic patients: neither group responds to REM sleep deprivation with the usual increase in REM time on recovery nights (Cartwright, Monroe, & Palmer, 1967; Cartwright & Ratzel, 1972). In waking, the NREM dreamer scores high on items designed to measure schizophrenia on personality tests (Foulkes, 1967; Cartwright & Ratzel, 1972). The failure of both groups to recoup lost REM time has pointed to the possibility that both the NREM dreamer and the schizophrenic have more permeable REM systems which allow dreamlike activity to occur in states other than REM when REM sleep is blocked. When this occurs, dreaming takes places outside REM, and no later REM-sleep rebound is needed to accommodate for the loss. Whether these dream intrusions into other states disrupt or enhance waking functioning depends on the mental health of the individual, what it is he has to express in those dreams, and how he uses this for increased creativity or chaos.

If dreaming and hallucinating arise from the same source, there are three ways this may be distributed: (1) dream-hallucinations may be narrowly confined to REM time, leaving NREM sleep and the focus of waking time for more conceptual, reality-oriented mental activity; (2) dreaming may occur more broadly in both REM and NREM sleep; or (3) it may occupy awareness sporadically throughout all three states. The first type of organization describes the distribution typical of most normal people most of the time; the second describes a small percentage of normals, maybe 10 to 15 percent, who are NREM dreamers either characteristically or perhaps only when they are under stress; and the third type is the actively hallucinating schizophrenic. What this all suggests is that the dispersion of this activity may make dream function less efficient.

Among the functions of dreaming that have been proposed, there is evidence that dreaming normally assimilates daytime feelings into memory networks which organize the personal implications of this experience and keep the sense of self intact (see Chapters 6 and 7). This appears to take the sting out of unpleasant and frightening experiences so that they can be coped with better in waking life. If dream symbols are the language for expressing the import to us of our waking experience, the directness and sterility of the dreams of schizophrenics may be an indication that this working through of emotion is not taking place. If this is so, the schizophrenic should be one who suffers from a poorly articulated conception of himself. His feeling-meanings will not mesh with his more cognitive meanings; the emotional component will remain isolated, and waking mastery of it will be poor. This lack of identity indeed seems to describe the schizophrenic in whom emotion is either dulled or bursts out, rather than being modulated appropriately.

## The Patient Study: Dreams and Stories

Much of this thinking is speculative. In order to test some of these ideas, we moved out of the university laboratory and onto the ward of a local psychiatric hospital where newly admitted, actively ill schizophrenic patients were kept drug-free for the first two weeks of their hospitalization. We worked with seven of these patients who were actively hallucinating during the day and one whose symptoms were improved. If waking hallucinations are escaped dreams, it seemed likely that the NREM sleep might also be harboring some of these escapees. To look into this, at least two REM and two NREM reports were collected for each patient. To get some comparable samples of waking thought, two story responses to TAT pictures were also requested, one the first thing in the morning after a night of uninterrupted sleep and the second at two o'clock in the afternoon on another day. To approximate a dream situation during the day, the story task was made an emotional problem situation to be solved. A picture was handed to the subject with these instructions:

> Here is someone in A LOT of trouble. Look at the picture and get it well in mind because I am going to ask you later what is the problem, and, if it were you, how would you solve it.

Before they went to sleep, the patients looked at a picture for a full minute. When they were awakened in the morning, they were asked:

> Do you remember the picture I showed you last night? What was the problem? How would you solve it if it were you?

To get the sample of the thought occurring later in the day, the alternate picture was shown when the subjects first woke up, and the resolution was requested seven hours later, at about two in the afternoon. Ten student subjects were selected that matched the patients in terms of age and of schizophrenia scores on a personality test (MMPI). Although not overtly ill these students had areas of disturbance like the patients. They also had two REM and two NREM sleep interruptions and gave story responses when they first woke up after an uninterrupted night of sleep.

Are the dreams from the REM periods of the patients less dreamlike than those of the students? Yes, they are. Only half of the reports from their REM awakenings had the qualities of a dream — that is, visual images which they accepted at the time as real. Despite the fact that half of these reports were "dreams," many of these were not at all bizarre, but really quite realistic. In fact, two-thirds of the patients' REM reports were everydayish in quality as opposed to less than half of those from the normals. The reports from the one patient whose symptoms were improved were more like those of the normals. Four out of his five dreams were of visual images he accepted as real.

The bare percentages do not convey the very big differences in just how "crazy" the dreams of the normal students sound in contrast to those of the patients. Most of the patients dreams were of home, work, and the hospital without much story development or abrupt change in time or place. The theme was usually a single statement: "I was at work, thinking about the good times I had there"; "I was in my room at home, feeling afraid"; "I saw a pass. I wondered whether my doctor would sign a pass for me to go on the picnic." These were not elaborated in terms of characters or plot, although there was usually at least one visual image involved. Only one out of all the REM reports from the acute patients really qualified as a "crazy" dream:

> I dreamt that I was in this classroom and the teacher dismissed the class and I got out of class. I walked out of the doorway and showed her the book as I walked out the door. And I walked in the hallways and I seen this friend of mine and I was walking down the highway and — I'd lost the book by then — and I noticed when I was walking down the street that it became a street in my hometown and I flew up on the top of this roof and it was the roof of a house that was shaped sort of like a giant tractor and I caved [in] the roof and the guy got out and got mad at me and I was trying to fly back of the garage to get away from him and then I woke up.

The "craziest" dream from the patient whose symptoms were improved was considerably more bizarre:

> I was dreaming I was with a friend. There was an ape loose in Brookfield Zoo that killed a girl. I had a pistol and the police framed us for murder. We had all of our privileges taken away and were told to leave the country. I had a weird fear of authority and felt guilt, anger, and hatred, and that it was not a free country. We walked through a department store, which was the border of the country. There we met a woman with seven or eight girls. The girls were also kicked out of the country for committing crimes. My friend and I decided how to split up the girls between us. He left with the girls to go to a house of prostitution and I stayed with a girl I used to know that was going to become a nun. We were by a bank of a creek and were cold and decided to build a fire. She was breaking up firewood and hit me with a twig. I hit her back and she was trying to start a log on fire without kindling wood and I was explaining to her that that cannot be done when I woke up.

In terms of the number of improbable events and abrupt changes of plot, this dream makes less logical sense than that of the most bizarre dream of an actively ill patient. Among the normal subjects, there were many dreams as bizarre as this one to choose from. The following one comes from the same time of night, 5:30 A.M., as the other two:

> I was driving this truck out of a parking lot. I'd been with an old girl friend of mine and she said . . . we were talking about each other, I guess, and I'm not sure what we were saying and she had other friends there and I was a little upset. One of these, one of her friends, it was kind of an older guy, he said, "Come on, we are going to have a dear cup of tea due to the kindness of a gay police lieutenant." During this time, we were walking around in the street someplace and the street turned into kind of a large parking lot which might be behind some buildings, not a huge one, not an industrial one, but a private residential parking lot. And there was a note with some instructions about how they had two truckloads of stuff to be taken someplace and one of them was to be hooked to the other somehow, and one truck was supposed to be hooked to the other, apparently through an electrical system. There were two drivers there, one of them, who was like the second in command, had hooked the two trucks together and the leader came over and said, "No, that's wrong because these trucks are the wrong kind of trucks and you can't do that with these." And he cut the lines with his hands like with a judo chop. Then he said, "OK" Then his truck became a Harley-Davidson Electroglide. And what he was going to do, I guess, was he was going to pull the other truck with it but it didn't seem like a good idea. I think there got to be a couple of extra trucks and one extra truck was my truck except it was like one of the original trucks hadn't turned into a motorcycle but a motorcycle had appeared and taken its place. I was in my truck and going to leave so I started to back up and my left rear wheel went off the downhill side of this parking lot onto the lawn and I was backing up until I could get my wheels back on the parking lot course so I could go forward. I was checking my mirrors and everything and I hit the uphill side of the parking lot and something cracked and it was the intercom and you calling me. The geography kept changing. I was walking up and down the street; sometimes we were sitting on a couch in a room, me and the old girl friend, mostly it took place on the street. In the dream there was a certain coarseness about her and I was really disillusioned about it and said to myself, "She's really not very attractive at all." I was still upset when these other friends came out.

In *content,* dreams reported from the REM periods of the patients sound more like the thoughts that drift through the mind before sleep than they do like dreams. They deal openly, although briefly, with real places and events. In fact, there was not much difference between their REM and NREM reports. In the *structure* of the thought and language, though, there was a great deal of difference between patients' REM and NREM reports and a marked difference between their reports and reports of normal subjects. The patients' REM reports were fraught with the signs of the thought disorder characteristic of schizophrenia.

### Schizophrenic Thought in the Three States

All the reports were scored on a scale designed to distinguish schizophrenic from nonschizophrenic verbal behavior (Gottschalk & Gleser, 1969). When the patients were awakened from REM, their language proved to be highly schizophrenic: full of incomplete sentences, garbled words, and repetitions. In fact, the scores on this scale of all the verbal samples from the patients—their REM and NREM reports and morning and afternoon stories —showed a U-shaped distribution (see Figure 6); that is they were high, then low, then high again. The reports from the REM awakenings were extremely high in terms of thought disruption. This was much less true of their reports from NREM sleep; in fact, some patients' scores for thought in NREM reports were within normal limits. In the morning, when they gave their story response to the picture, all patients' verbal behavior was so low it fell within the normal range of scores. By 2:00 P.M.,

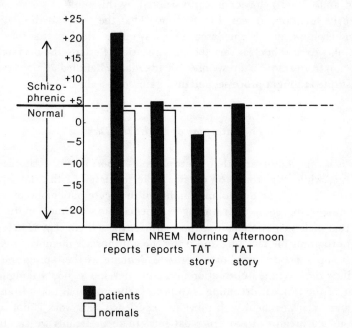

FIGURE 6. Schizophrenia scores for fantasy in sleep and waking periods of patients and normal subjects

when the second story was requested, the group average was again high enough to be over the border of being "schizophrenic."

What about the normals? When they report their bizarre dreams from REM sleep, do they also think and talk like schizophrenics? Perhaps just being awakened abruptly over an intercom by a stranger in the middle of the night is enough to make anyone's thought style rather disjointed. It is interesting that although the average scores for both the REM and NREM reports of the normal subjects were normal, this is where they were most like schizophrenics; five of the ten had slightly abnormal scores for their REM reports. It seems that the thought disruption characteristic of schizophrenia has a waxing and waning course over the time periods we sampled here. The high point for both groups was reached during REM reporting. This suggests that the reorientation of attention required to communicate dream experience is very disruptive, although much more so for schizophrenics than for normals. Both groups had the second highest disruption level in the NREM awakenings. Morning was the "low" point; in terms of articulation, none of the patients' stories was scored as schizophrenic when they first awoke. This may mean that at the point of awakening the sleeper's attention is ready for engagement with the outside world and verbal behavior is not disrupted by this shift. If so, sleep has served its function, at least for the time. That the scores of the patients again become schizophrenic later in the day reflects the fact that they lack the ability to sustain clear verbal communication. Perhaps the demand for attention from emotional responses not adequately handled at night results in disrupted thought processes and disorganized speech.

### The Interplay of Night and Day

Why is it that the dreams that schizophrenics report sound so simple and realistic, while the stories or dreams collected later in the day are so bizarre? This may be due to an inability of the acute patients to organize their inner responses to their waking experience into some meaningful pattern that makes emotional sense and reaffirms the self-concept. Their personal programs for recalling and using the appropriate memories needed to develop a good dream may be as inadequate as their programs for handling the daytime information needed to develop a good waking idea. If one of the tasks of dreaming is to process the marginal notes from the day and integrate them with previous experience, this work is not being done in the dreams of the acute patients. In their dreams we can often recognize leftover elements of reality from the day as well as some feelings, but rarely does the dream mill grind out a complicated scenario that associates this to its larger context of meaning in their lives. Their dreams fail to work out analogies that would give emotional continuity to their experience or any opportunity for reviewing how problems have been mastered in the past. Every dream in the night of a schizophrenic, in other words, sounds like one from a first REM period. A problem is stated, but something prevents the development of more complicated dreams that ordinarily takes place as REM periods become longer. There is no continuity of theme from REM to REM across the night; dream thought is as disorganized as waking thought.

If dreaming is an ongoing stream of mental activity which surfaces to command attention when the conditions are right, the conditions are never quite right for the acute schizophrenic while asleep. In sleep, his REM state is fragmented rather than sustained, and his eye movements are too few (Feinberg et al., 1965; Lairy, Barros-Ferreira, & Goldsteinas, 1968). He experiences poorly developed, minimal dreams. The acute schizophrenic's characteristic difficulty in voluntarily controlling attention during waking allows dreamlike activity to erupt into daytime thought. Since the emotions of the previous waking experience have not been integrated and defused, when they obtrude into the waking state as hallucinations or directly in behavior they are extreme and inappropriate. In contrast, the chronic (long-term) schizophrenic is often characterized by emotional "flatness," as if his failure adequately to assimilate emotions in dreams over a long period of time has left his waking psyche divorced from this material and his sense of self unsure.

How may this tentative knowledge be used to help the schizophrenic patient? Vogel and Traub (1968) once attempted to approach the problem of getting a little life into chronic schizophrenics by REM-depriving them. Their thinking was that this procedure would force material from dreams into waking behavior, giving the psychiatrist something more to work with productively by day. This brave attempt was a failure. Nothing happened, probably because nothing was happening in the patients' dreams, either. We might better tackle the problem the other way round: suppress waking hallucinations in order to force more active dreaming. The trick is to do this without the use of REM-suppressing medications, not a possibility at present.

Inefficient dreaming is not the only thing wrong with schizophrenics, but eliminating daytime hallucinations would make it easier to work with and help these people. Our "crazy" dreams may not be what keep us sane, but when our dreams are well developed and dealing with our feelings, our

waking sense of who we are and our behavior are generally better integrated. Dreaming is a creative response to what is happening now which
draws on all of our personal history. This appears to serve adaptive (useful)
functions which are lacking in the waking hallucinator—primarily to
reconcile the present with the past and to try out some consequences in fantasy. All of this aids our ability to face the world with a steady sense of self.

# Nine

# THE PLACE OF DREAMING IN OUR PSYCHOLOGICAL BALANCE

Examing the thought operations of our night life to help illuminate our understanding of the mind of man has a long tradition. Dreaming is such a familiar and yet mysterious phenomenon that many explanations have been offered to account for it. Much of this work has concentrated on understanding "what" is dreamed. The interest in this book is directed less to that question than to the questions "why" we dream and "how" this relates to the rest of experience. The development of laboratory methods of monitoring the sleeping brain make it possible now to translate many ideas about dreaming into propositions that can be systematically tested. The methods of science can now be used to weigh these propositions and find if they are supported by the rules of evidence.

### Freud's View

The three giants of psychiatry, Freud, Jung, and Adler, had quite different views of dreaming and of its relation to waking mental life. These have been elaborated and amended over the years in the works of others, yet all three are still recognizably distinct. Freud gave special emphasis in his dream theory to the observation that sleep is a time of minimal physical action. Because of this, there is less need to hold back the primitive impulses which, he argued, supply the energy behind our waking actions. In fact, dreaming allows us safely to gratify these unacceptable wishes. In sleep, drives repressed by day are allowed expression, although the gratification is only an illusion. Even though sleep protects us from blame or guilt, these deep-rooted wishes are so repulsive to our waking selves that even the dream images cannot be direct and open expressions of what we want. Instead, they are symbols — compromises between the unconscious wishes and the conscious restraining forces.

According to this view, which has come to be known as the "complementarity" position, there is an equalizing effect between the opposing forces guiding waking and sleeping mental life, which is why dreams are so foreign to us: they represent the expression and gratification of unfamiliar, denied impulses, and do so in indirect language.

### Adler's View

To Adler, dreams are not in opposition to the thought of waking life, but a continuation of it. They are a product of our lifestyle, an attempt to resolve present problems by supporting the style, or personality, of the dreamer as he pursues his goals. The specific task of dreaming, according to Adler, is to prepare the person's feelings that will accompany his realistic actions the next day. The actual solutions to problems worked out in dreams may well be nonsensical but they are not the important things either to remember or use. It is the feelings they arouse which are useful to our waking purposes. To Adler, dreams have a "future orientation" arising out of unfinished business: they deal with problems not yet solved. Dreams offer trial solutions which, like the metaphors used by a poet, are intended more to create emotion which fires us to act than as direct bases for specific actions. The way dreams manage this "continuation" of work on waking problems is by reaffirming the dreamer's lifestyle. The content of dreams is unimportant; it is their feelings that effect subsequent waking behavior.

### Jung's View

For Jung, dreams confront us with personal concerns presently most in need of waking adjustment. The function is one of "balancing" or compensation to maintain or restore harmony to the whole being. A dream represents not just our conscious problems or unconscious wishes, but the whole personality, and behaves accordingly to regulate inner harmony. In other words, if our waking behavior is in keeping with our whole nature, then our dreams might well resemble our waking thoughts; but if our behavior distorts the essential character of our being, then there will be outbreaks of bad dreams, illness, neurotic disorders, and bad moods. Under these circumstances, dreams provide us with clues to what we need to bring back into balance to restore smooth functioning. For Jung, the relation of dreaming to waking life is continuous when all is well, and complementary at other times in areas where the waking personality is not representative of the whole person.

## The Adaptive Function of Mind: Waking

Freud, Adler, and Jung all constructed their theories by analyzing the dreams of people seeking their help for personal difficulties. As psychiatrists, these men worked at understanding the person from the dreams, using their knowledge of their patients' waking mental life one by one. Their generalizations into theory came later. More recent dream theories (Breger, 1969; Shapiro, 1967) are attempts to apply general models of waking thought constructed from experimental studies to the mental life of sleep. Piaget (1963), Gibson (1966), and Neisser (1967), for example, have offered explanations about how the waking mind works based on their studies of normal persons. To put the research on dreaming and waking together for a round-the-clock model of the mind is a major challenge to present-day psychology.

The idea behind this effort is that mind, as we know it during waking, has an *adaptive* function—that is, it is keyed to dealing effectively with reality. It is likely, therefore, that nighttime mental activity also serves some purpose. Comparing the nature of the two types of activity yields hunches to be explored and relationships to be tested. The statement that the mind has an adaptive function means that mental activity allows behavior to be flexible in a way that frees us from the demands of the moment. Because we can draw on past experiences and anticipate the future, we have a greater choice of responses. The basic mechanism underlying flexible behavior is the fact that the nervous system itself is changed by experience. Our nervous system constantly compares new experiences with our memory or internal model of the same or similar experiences. In this way, we consciously and unconsciously make predictions of consequences and adjust our behavior appropriately with reference to this stored representation of experience. If consequences do not gibe with our prediction, we alter the internal model that represents it to incorporate the new experience. We do not, however, store or retrieve our information exactly as it was experienced. Memory is a creative process. What is stored is not a photographic replica of the original, and what is recalled is also a creation based on what was stored. Modifications are made according to the current situation and present needs.

Waking behavior is more appropriate, and serves us better, the better our capacity to extract information in the present and integrate it with previously stored information. This information comes from three sources: information which is new may be derived either from present internal or external sources; old information comes from memory. There is always more information available than we can attend to, since the capacity for full attention is limited. To insure an efficient selection process internal rules or schemata are developed to handle information in a shorthand way. These do not always work well. Some may be poorly suited to adaptation, as is the case in phobias, stereotypes, and prejudices. These organize new information, but in an inflexible way that limits the individual's behavioral opportunities because he makes inappropriate generalizations (stereotypes), sees dangers where none exist (phobias), and suffers from less adaptive behavior.

The information in the spotlight of attention can be there either by active choice or because it impresses us with its strength or novelty or for some other reason. The material we pay attention to in waking thought is strongly characterized by choice. We can turn our minds at will to any of the three sources. Attending to the present external source, I may notice the yellow traffic light and the time on my watch; attending to internal feelings, I notice a sense of tension and hurry; attending to my memory schema for these experiences, I recall that it was at this corner that I got a ticket for entering an intersection on a yellow light when I felt hurried. All of this information input and retrieval can happen very quickly and determine the adaptive behavior of braking to a stop.

The thoughts that we do not choose to have but which are impressed upon us can also come from internal or external sources, such as noticing the internal urgency feelings that accompany a full bladder or the external ringing of the phone or, worst of all, both at the same time. During waking, the memory store source does not often have the same power to command attention in an unintentional way, except under unusual circumstances. Obsessive memories can occur after an upsetting experience or during a period of stress when a reverberating circuit seems to get set in motion. Then, without choice, we relive memories over and over that we would rather not.

## The Adaptive Function of Mind: Sleeping

How does all of this relate to the mental activity of sleep? Do dream thoughts have the same characteristics and function? There are several marked differences. One is that during sleep the voluntary character of thought is lost. Dreams are rarely chosen; most often they are impressed upon us. Another difference is that unlike waking thoughts, dreams rarely represent present external or internal information. Predominantly, they come from recent and long-term memory sources in creative new combinations. This would class them as being unbidden memories, which are rare by day. Therefore, the elements that go to make up a dream are different than most of our waking thoughts.

During waking, the first operation performed on the information that is in the focus of awareness is to "recognize" it—that is, to assimilate it to the appropriate memory organization or accommodate a schema to fit a new experience. Most simply this is done by one of two methods. The baby does his first recognizing by matching a memory image to the present external stimulus without the use of language. This happens when the sight of a bottle is enough to stop the crying. The next recognition style the child develops is naming; for example, he calls all four-footed creatures "dog." We make errors as we use both of these techniques, but usually there is some feedback from reality to correct this process as it occurs.

After the initial step of recognizing, information may undergo more complicated processing into storage. This is not always completed at sleep onset. When an experience arouses strong feelings, or is so novel that no present schema is adequate to handle it, or when we are distracted by a competing stimulus before we finish the assimilation, a tension system is left open. In these cases, the processing of this material until it is resolved continues in sleep.

This appears to be particularly true for the more subjective internal information—the new feelings and fantasies that arise in the course of daily life and the old ones that are revived. Schemata for organizing this kind of internal information are usually cruder and more poorly articulated than are those by which objectively observable external information is handled. We have been taught how to organize our perceptions of the world: what and how to see. We have not been taught (by parents, teachers, etc.) how to order our inner experience, nor have we been en-couraged to refine our processing of it, either by identifying and naming the beast, or by matching the shades of feelings to previous ones. This leaves this material, even when we do attend to it directly, often in-completely processed at nightfall.

Most frequently, of course, we do not give this information our full at-tention by day. It is not often that we sit down and ask ourselves what is it that we feel, unless we are in therapy. This usually takes place only on the edges of our awareness — in the preconscious, or unconscious — and this is the material of the dream-stream. Such material is processed quite crude-ly, usually without the need for corrections even being noted at the time. If these inner stimuli are strong enough and strike at our important sense of self (like the feelings of anxiety aroused in Jerry and Don by being sleep ex-periment subjects), or if they are labeled in passing as important thoughts to get back to, they seem to go into a buffer store, a sort of holding area, until the high arousal state of REM sleep, when they impress themselves upon our attention as dream images. In this way, there is a continuous pro-cessing of feelings by assimilation to older memory schemata. This is a longer, much slower process than the information encoding, storage, and retrieval of external information because there is less need for immediate action. Two separate systems seem to be involved: one that maps the in-formation relevant to the world around us, and the other which is our per-sonal map of who we are.

The mind has two major methods for processing data into and out of both storage systems. The first is *perceptual experiencing*; this begins with imaging, using images for recognizing. The second is *conceptual thinking*; this begins, using verbal symbols, with naming. These terms bear some relation to the two thought styles Freud described as "primary process" and "secondary process," and to those called by others "holistic" and "linear." They also seem to be functionally related to different brain locations, the right and left hemispheres. Although both appear to contribute to the mental activity that takes place during sleep and waking, they differ in proportion in these different states. The secondary-process or conceptual mode is more in evidence during waking, when reality, language, and logic must prevail in our communications with others and interactions with the world. The left hemisphere is specialized for these tasks. The primary-process, perceptual mode is more characteristic of dreaming, when the need to make sense to others is low and imagination and emotion can hold sway. The right hemisphere is more specialized in this activity. These describe the extremes, but in fact we operate in both modes rather con-tinuously with a difference only in emphasis, depending in part on the demands of the task at hand—say, drawing a picture versus doing addition.

Although the primary dream mode is the perceptual, the conceptual is not completely inoperative in sleep. A good deal of talking goes on between the characters in most dreams, although it may be a bit bizarre. This thought style is also characteristic of mental content during NREM sleep as it takes place between dreams. These thoughts may be an intermediate step between waking experiences and dreams. They may influence directly the choice of the images to be triggered in the next REM episode.

In waking, too, we are not always operating in just one mode. There are stable individual differences that make one style more prominent than the other. Some persons characteristically attend more to external stimuli, while others are more generally internally responsive. There is also the possibility that the ninety-minute rhythm which brings us into the imagistic dreaming mode regularly throughout the night also operates during waking. It is likely that during the day, when more voluntary control is possible, this tendency for a shift of attention to subjective stimuli every ninety minutes can be overridden, but only with effort. During times of more passive pursuits such as listening to lectures or reading on one's own, the shift may occur more easily than when we are performing a task requiring that we make regular active responses. This waking shift of focus may occur more often than every ninety minutes, but it appears to become imperative that attention shift on that schedule. At these times, there is a difference not only in the source of the thoughts, but often also in the method by which they are processed. We are less likely to be logically "thinking about" an internal or external event and more likely to be "imagining-as-if." However, while awake, we have the power to control the direction these thoughts take in both modes. In fact, it is hard for us to give up control on demand. We have to be taught to "free-associate" in psychoanalysis, for example. Typically, we stop one train of thought and start another if it does not please us or meet our tests of reality. We can even say of a daydream, "I know it can never happen, but wouldn't it be great if . . ." and choose not to stop, but to continue an imaginary sequence.

In general, except for these fantasy breaks, waking thought is primarily directed toward monitoring information from the objective world around us, toward moving such information into and out of memory stores as needed so that we may get on with the activities necessary to daily life. During dreaming, stimuli go mostly one way: they are not as often received as retrieved. The experiences of the day come out of their holding pattern according to the organizational schema that represents their

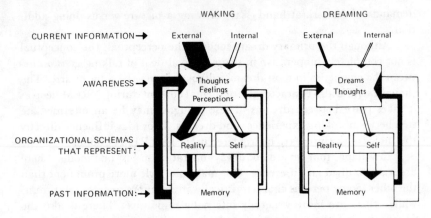

FIGURE 7.  The sources of thoughts in waking and dreaming

relevance to the self and bring with them related images from past experiences. (See Figure 7.)

Another difference between waking and dreaming thought is that when the processing of a waking experience is continued in dreams, it is done by way of an involuntary organization of perceptual images without the feedback of any reality. There is no external check on their validity to correct errors of perception.

## Does This Model Fit the Data?

One question this thinking suggests is: Since we have choice both of what to think about and how to think about it in waking time, and since attention needs to be balanced, do differences in the way we distribute our waking attention have different consequences for our dream life? We might expect those persons who, because of occupation or temperament, give more attention to external stimuli, and to the processing of these in the reality-oriented, left-brained, logical mode, to experience a clearer difference between their waking thoughts and their dreams. Their dreams may be of the "wild beast" nature in which all the unattended private world must be given its due. This was suggested as an explanation for the difference between the dreams of the husband and wife reported in Chapter 3. Liz, who dealt with language and abstractions all day, cherished her long, complicated dream plots. These were rich in feeling and visual symbolic material. Ken, who worked by day creating images directly in clay, rarely recalled his dreams, which were shorter, calmer, and simpler. Similarly, in

Chapter 4 the students in the REM-deprivation study whose personality tests showed them to be externally balanced, who attend more to stimuli from without than to those from within, responded to the loss of dream opportunity with a shift of attention toward more internal stimuli. Those students whose daytime attention was nearly more equally balanced did not have a shift in style with REM loss.

On a larger scale, our whole culture has overstressed practicality, reality orientation, and secondary-process logic as the most valued uses of mind and method to solve problems. Beginning in the mid-1960s, there was a massive reaction to this. One form this took was that many people began to seek more direct contact with others through encounters mediated, not by language, but by touch, as well as with themselves, mediated by drugs or special techniques to block the external sources of thought. The boom in meditation and biofeedback training resulted. Jung would say we had become too one-sided and were distorting our natures, not living in the wholeness of our potential. When dreams cannot take up all the slack, there are outbreaks in our waking behavior of deliberate experiments in expanding awareness of inner experiencing. This reasoning presupposes that there is a natural balance of attention to internal and external data and of the operation in both thought modes over the twenty-four hours.

If this reasoning is sound, persons who deliberately close off their attention to external information during waking with regular periods of meditation might be expected to have a reduced need for dreaming or a different proportion of REM to NREM sleep than those who are bombarded with extra loads of sensory input.

One of our students looked into this by studying the sleep of a group of experienced Divine Light meditators and a group of novices who had not yet begun to practice this technique (Butters, 1976). Both groups spent an hour before sleep in a special activity. The meditators sat with eyes closed and concentrated on their breathing, an inner light, and the taste of a sweet fluid. The novices sat with eyes closed and stereo headphones on, listening to music. The meditators' sleep records were in no way different from normal. Withdrawing attention in this way did not result in less REM time.

The sleep records of the novices did show a big effect. Their REM time was distinctly elevated. An hour's worth of concentrated attention on external auditory stimulation just prior to sleep was followed by more REM. Meditation does not substitute for REM. It may be refreshing and anxiety-reducing, but it does not accomplish the processing of internal responses which is the psychological work of REM.

Was the increase in REM in the novice group a response to the increase in external stimulation in general, or was it specific to the kind of stimulation? Music is processed in the right hemisphere and may have overstimulated that system. Tracing this down is an area of current research. Before saying that meditation has no effect on our night life, not just the REM time but the dreams, too, should be explored. These may be calmer and happier than those of the person whose waking cognitive life is thoroughly engaged in the struggle with the outer world.

The factor controlling the content of dreams and determining which memory stores furnish dream materials may be as Adler would have it, the need to complete or reach closure on the uncompleted business of the day relevant to our lifestyle. As we have seen, the night's first dream is usually a continuation of a current conscious concern, or one which has been waiting in the wings of the preconscious or unconscious for its turn in the spotlight. The images which emerge to illustrate and elaborate it are associated by analogy, by similarity or contrast of feelings, or by some simple spatial or temporal association. Dreams are drawn from the inner responses to experiences which have received too little attention, either because of emotional reasons, as Freud might view it, or simply because that is a more efficient use of time. With the release of the voluntary control of attention to external affairs that comes with sleep, the mind shifts to this unfinished content. When we are functioning well enough to be aware of what is happening in both our objective and subjective experience—to be open to our awareness, as Rogers (1959) would say—there may not be as much work left undone that dreams need to continue. In this case, we might be freer to use our dreams to create and to play, as the Senoi are said to do.

None of the three major dream theories from the world of psychiatry has been disproven by the experimental work in sleep. In fact, all have received some support. Dreaming appears to be continuous in terms of supporting the lifestyle or ego of the dreamer, particularly when this is under threat; to be complementary in expressing the emotional side of experience that is underrepresented in waking mental life; and to operate in the normal person to make him whole again, to center him when his balance has been upset during the day. Still, these statements are all rather vague and imprecise. The concluding chapter will be more specific in stating what we know about dream functions based on recent experimental evidence.

# Ten

# THE USEFULNESS OF DREAMING

### *Are Dreams Useful?*

We have asked many questions about dreaming and explored some of the evidence currently available to provide the answers. The most central of these questions is whether this mental activity, so long ignored by academic and research psychologists, serves some important function.

### DREAMS HAVE MEANING

Any group of dreams collected on one laboratory night from the same person makes such a coherent statement that it is hard to entertain the idea that these are random events. The dreams of a night constitute a body of thought in which each has meaning singly; but more important, they form an interrelated whole. As a group, they reflect the dreamer's personal responses to waking life and relate these responses to the remembered past and to the hopes and fears of the future. What is more, they do this regularly each night throughout the life span.

Although we do not know precisely at what age dreaming begins, there is no doubt that this is very early. The two-year-old who wakes one morning, gets out of bed, and hits her sleeping sister "because," as she explains, "she was being so mean to me," is responding to a dream. Children soon learn the difference between dreams and waking reality, and to divorce the two. Only some primitive people hold others responsible for what they dream about them. In this culture, children quickly learn that dreams have an internal origin and are taught firmly to discount the information they contain.

## DREAMS ARE INSISTENT

It is obvious that some function is served by this experience when we consider the insistence with which dreaming occurs in spite of all attempts to prevent it. If aborted through the interruption or suppression of REM sleep, it will either occur with increased frequency and intensity in NREM sleep or redirect waking attention and thought to include more subjective responses. If waking fantasy is encouraged during the time when night dreams usually occur, less recuperation of the REM time lost will follow. If waking fantasy is prevented during the usual time for dreams, an increase in REM time will follow. All of this adds up to the statement that dreaming is an important part of human psychology.

## DREAMS INDICATE PSYCHOLOGICAL IMBALANCE

The facts that dreams are common, have meaning, and are a persistent phenomenon are not proof they have a usefulness in maintaining psychological balance. The finding that acute schizophrenics, whose waking behavior is so clearly unbalanced, are poor dreamers lends some weight to this possibility, however. The ability to have emotional, unrealistic, image-filled dreams seems to be part of normal behavior. It is not the failure to have "crazy" dreams that makes schizophrenics bizarre by day, but their difficulty controlling their own attention. They are unable to focus on either external realities or internal fantasies for very long without one intruding on the other. This makes their ability to extract relevant information and integrate it poor both in waking and sleep. There is something healthy about the voluntary nature of perception and thought during waking and its involuntary character in sleep, features lacking in these people.

## How Are Dreams Useful?

To demonstrate the usefulness of dreaming, let's discuss three major psychological areas — attention, affect, and cognition — and how dreaming affects them.

### ATTENTION

The psychological usefulness of this balance between waking and sleeping mental life was partly illustrated in the REM-deprivation studies we have discussed. First, and most generally, dreaming has effects on waking attention. When it has taken place, we awake ready to shift attention to active engagement with reality. When it has not, our focus of attention drifts back to subjective inner material. Of course, an individual does not have to be dream-deprived or psychotic in order to pay attention to imaginative thoughts and inner feelings during waking. This is usually a matter of choice. Lapses that are unintentional only happen in the normal person when stimulus levels are lower or higher than usual, when we are affected by the monotony of a long-distance drive or when we get that buried-alive feeling when a lecturer throws too much information at us too rapidly. In neither the intended nor unintended instances are the experiences as compelling as the dreams of nighttime, when we are totally and uncritically involved. In the normal person, waking and sleeping fantasies are different in character. Waking fantasies are more voluntary not only regarding time of occurrence, but also in terms of their duration and subject matter. We never lose track of the "as-if" character of a daydream; we know it is a fancy we are indulging. In dreams, we are taken in completely, conned by our own unconscious. This seems to keep attention clear for voluntary control by day.

### AFFECT

A second effect of dreaming demonstrated through its loss is on *affect*, or feelings. Dreams appear to regulate the subjective world of feelings and help us adapt to stressful experiences so that we can handle them more realistically during waking. Dreams represent feeling-laden material relevant to our sense of self from experiences of the past few days being assimilated into their proper association networks. If the material does not fit well, the personal program may not operate to run the data through in the usual way, but tend to repeat steps until some resolution or accommodation can be reached.

Of the dreams we have discussed, Jerry's and Don's (Chapter 2), Ken's (Chapter 3), and the medical students' and gay students' (Chapter 6) all illustrate how dream images match whatever uneasy feelings we have that are related to the self and that are aroused prior to sleep. As the night progresses, these images are followed by dreams that incorporate past instances involving similar feelings. This continues until there is a clear statement of the problem: how to reconcile this experience with our model of the self. At this point, there may be a dream with marked contrast in feeling. The feeling-meaning aroused in response to waking experience is explored widely in dreams in the context of the whole life history of the dreamer. The type of thinking is exploratory unless the waking threat to the self is very strong, and then our dream thoughts converge in defense of the self. In the normal person, dreams serve to help us work out our problem feelings. They lead to calmer, more realistic handling of a specific instance in which emotion was aroused in waking, at least until there is a new instance. Even the nightmare can act like a good Greek tragedy to purge our fears.

## COGNITION

The third area of dream function explored in the laboratory in recent years is the usefulness of dreaming in cognition, or thinking. This includes studies of the effects of memory and ability to solve problems. Attempts have been made to show that dreams not only housekeep to tidy up the personal leftovers, turn down tempers, and prepare the sleeper for attention to reality the next day, but that they also plan strategies that will improve conscious thought processes. Here the studies are few and not so clear. The style of thought in dreaming is certainly different, but there is little current evidence that dreams lead directly to more information or better answers unless they are first decoded in consciousness.

The question of the usefulness of dreams must be addressed as a two-part question:

1. What useful functions do dreams perform on their own, without the collaboration of the waking mind?

2. What useful functions can dreams perform with the aid of conscious understanding of the content?

## What Dreams Do on Their Own

The answer to the first part of our question has been discussed. As for the second part, dreaming appears to be involved in the balance of attention. The voluntary control and focus of the kind of attention during waking that is necessary for doing what we want done comes about through an internal alternation mechanism which may depend on a regular shift in the dominance of the two brain hemispheres from left ("realistic"/daytime/ waking) to right ("imagistic"/nighttime/dreaming) and back again. Dreaming also appears to handle the feeling responses from the previous day. This comes about through the assimilation of present subjective responses into the context of their personal implications. This works differently in different individuals depending on how aware and tolerant they are of their inner life in waking. The less in touch a person is with this internal information, the stronger his dream feelings will have to be to restore psychological balance. The more self-knowledge a person has and the more open to his feelings in waking, the less adjusting of feelings his dreams will have to do.

## What Dreams Might Do, with Awareness

The psychotherapist knows that uncovering dream meanings can have very real effects on a patient's waking life. If, through the laboratory method, persons could gain waking command of a large body of this material, would they be more frightened or enlightened? Freud would argue that recall by itself does not necessarily bring about understanding except on a superficial basis. Dreams are disguised for a reason and should remain so. Furthermore, any deep understanding without careful preparation could overwhelm the individual. The Jungians disagree. Carl Meier (1969) says that if this were ture, we would have subjects running screaming from the laboratory. Perhaps the fact that this does not actually happen, is because subjects do not "understand" the deeper meaning of their dreams. To which Jung (1968) would answer, "the dream does not conceal; we simply do not understand the language" (p. 92). He said further, "Dreams are as simple or as complicated as the dreamer is himself only they are always a little bit ahead of the dreamer's consciousness. I do not understand my own dreams any better than any of you for they are always beyond my grasp. . . . Knowledge is no advantage when it is a matter of one's own dreams" (p. 122).

If dreams are difficult to understand only because the language is foreign to us—our forgotten language, Fromm (1951) calls it—can we become bilingual if we start learning in early childhood, before we are trained to forget? When a child calls in the middle of the night, "I'm frightened!" the parent usually turns on the light and says, "See, there is nothing to be afraid of. It was only something you dreamed. Go back to sleep and forget it." What if instead the parent said to the child, "Tell me about it," and listened to the dreamstory with interest and care? Part of the child's fear would be reduced immediately by the sharing experience. If the parent then responded, "That was an interesting story you were telling yourself," the child would feel rewarded and also would recognize that the dream was his own, not something being done to him; he would take a different attitude toward it. When the parent then asks, "I wonder why you were telling yourself this story?" the stage is set for curiosity to take the place of fear, rejection, and alienation from the dream life.

When children are very young, parents are in a position to know about almost all the waking experiences that might influence the dream-formation process: the daytime frustrations and upsets, the TV images they have seen and fairytale themes they have heard. All of these appear quite openly. And in fact the dreams of children are rather simple. When they are shared and it becomes a game to decode them, parents and children can both learn from the process and develop a special kind of closeness. This does not have to be done daily to have an effect on the child's ability to develop the concepts necessary to better understand his dreams and himself. The occasional sharing of the work on a particularly puzzling or intriguing dream is enough to open this door to self-knowledge. The usefulness of dreams in this regard is an untapped resource at this time. If youngsters grew up differently, not divorced from their subjective world of inner responses as too many are now, but gaining the ability to translate from the imagistic language to the conceptual, to refine the way their feelings and fantasies are organized to form the self, they might live more wholly, in better touch with themselves.

The study of the nature and function of our "night life" might well prepare us for this better day. This is, after all, the goal of psychotherapy; a wider sense of self, the ability to bring into awareness the inner responses as they occur and to integrate feeling and action in current behavior. How much better it would be to grow up so well that psychotherapy would not be needed later to reacquaint us with ourselves. The possibility of this kind of usefulness is what keeps the night lights burning in the sleep laboratory. Aside from the hope of this distant goal, there is a need for many studies to fill out our present knowledge and test our understanding of the mind of man as it functions throughout the sequence of day into night into day.

# REFERENCES

ABOOD, L., & BIEL, J. Anticholinergic psychotomemetic agents. *International Review of Neurobiology*, 1962, *4*, 217 -273.

ADLER, A. On the interpretation of dreams. *International Journal of Individual Psychology*, 1936, *1*, 3-16.

ALLEN, S., OSWALD, I., LEWIS, S., & TAGNEY, J. The effects of distorted visual input on sleep. *Psychophysiology, 1972, 9*, 498-504.

ANTROBUS, J.S., ANTROBUS, J., & FISHER, C. Discrimination of dreaming and non-dreaming sleep. *Archives of General Psychiatry*, 1965, *12*, 395-401.

AREY, L. *Clinical state and dream-sleep patterns of reactive schizophrenics.* Paper presented to the Association for Psychophysiological Study of Sleep, Palo Alto, Calif., 1964.

ASERINSKY, E., & KLEITMAN, N. Regularly occurring periods of eye motility and concommitant phenomena during sleep. *Science*, 1953, *118*, 273.

BARKER, R. The effects of REM sleep on the retention of a visual task. *Psychophysiology*, 1972, *9*, 107.

BERGER, R. The sleep and dream cycle. In A. Kales (Ed.), *Sleep: Physiology and pathology.* Philadelphia: Lippincott, 1969. (a)

BERGER, R. Ocularmotor control: A possible function of REM sleep. *Psychological Review*, 1969, *76*, 144-164. (b)

BERGER, R., & OSWALD, I. Eye movements during active and passive dreams. *Science*, 1962, *137*, 601.

BERLUCCHI, F. Callosal activity in unrestrained unanesthetized cats. *Archives Italiennes de Biologie*, 1965, *103*, 623-634.

BERTINI, M., GREGOLINI, H., & VITALI, S. Dream research: a new experimental approach. *Psychophysiology*, 1972, *9*, 115.

BLOCK, J. *The Q sort method in personality assessment and psychiatric research.* Springfield, Ill.: Thomas, 1961.

BOKERT, E. The effects of thirst and a related verbal stimulus on dream reports. *Dissertation Abstracts*, 1968, *28*, 122-131.

BREGER, L. Dream function: An information processing model. In L. Breger (Ed.), *Clinical-cognitive psychology.* Englewood Cliffs, N.J.: Prentice-Hall, 1969.

BREGER, L., HUNTER, I., & LANE, R. The effect of stress on dreams. *Psychological Issues*, 1971, *7*, Monograph 27.

BUTTERS, E., The effects of Divine Light Meditation on some electrophysiological indices of sleep. Paper presented to the Association for the Psychopsysiological Study of Sleep, Cincinnati, 1976.

CARRINGTON, P. Dreams and schizophrenia. *Archives of General Psychiatry*, 1972, *26*, 343-350.

CARTWRIGHT, R. Dream and drug-induced fantasy behavior. *Archives of General Psychiatry*, 1966, *15*, 7-15.

CARTWRIGHT, R. Sleep fantasy in normal and schizophrenic persons. *Journal of Abnormal Psychology*, 1972, *80*, 275-279.

CARTWRIGHT, R. Problem solving: Waking and dreaming. *Journal of Abnormal Psychology*, 1974, *83*, 451-455.

CARTWRIGHT, R. The influence of a conscious wish on dreams. *Journal of Abnormal Psychology*, 1974, *83*, 387-393.

CARTWRIGHT, R., BERNICK, N., BOROWITZ, G., & KLING, A. The effect of an erotic movie on the sleep and dreams of young men. *Archives of General Psychiatry*, 1969, *20*, 262-271.

CARTWRIGHT, R., LLOYD, S., BUTTERS, L., WEINER, L., MCCARTHY, L., & HANCOCK, J. The effects of REM time on what is recalled. *Psychophysiology*, 1975, *12*, 149-159.

CARTWRIGHT, R., & MONROE, L. The relation of dreaming and REM sleep: The effects of REM deprivation under two conditions. *Journal of Personality and Social Psychology*, 1968, *10*, 69-74.

CARTWRIGHT, R., MONROE, L., & PALMER, C. Individual differences in response to REM deprivation. *Archives of General Psychiatry*, 1967, *16*, 297-303.

CARTWRIGHT, R., & RATZEL, R. Effects of dream loss on waking behaviors. *Archives of General Psychiatry*, 1972, *27*, 277-280.

CASTALDO, V. Down's syndrome: A study of sleep patterns related to level of mental retardation. *American Journal of Mental Deficiency*, 1969, *74*, 187.

CASTALDO, V., & KRYNICKI, V. Sleep pattern and intelligence in functional mental retardation. *Journal of Mental Deficiency*, 1973, *17*, 231-235.

CLAUSEN, J., SERSEN, E., & LIDSKY, A. Variability of sleep measures in normal subjects. *Psychophysiology*, 1974, *11*, 509-516.

D'ANDRADE, R. The effect of culture on dreams. In F. Hsu (Ed.), *Psychological anthropology: Approaches to culture and personality*. Homewood, Ill.: Dorsey, 1961.

DEMENT, W. Dream recall and eye movements during sleep in schizophrenics and normals. *Journal of Nervous and Mental Disease*, 1955, *122*, 263-269.

DEMENT, W. The effect of dream deprivation. *Science*, 1960, *131*, 1705.

DEMENT, W. The biological role of REM sleep (circa 1968). In A. Kales (Ed.), *Sleep physiology and pathology*. Philadelphia: Lippincott, 1969.

DEMENT, W. *Some must watch while some must sleep*. San Francisco: Freeman, 1974.

DEMENT, W. & KLEITMAN, N. Relation of eye movements during sleep to dream activity: Objective method for study of dreaming. *Journal of Experimental Psychology*, 1957, *53*, 339-346. (a)

DEMENT, W. & KLEITMAN, N. Cyclic variations in EEG during sleep and their relation to eye movements, body motility, and dreaming. *Electroencephalography and Clinical Neurophysiology*, 1957, *9*, 673-690 (b)

DEMENT, W., & WOLPERT, E. The relation of eye movements, body motility, and external stimuli to dream content. *Journal of Experimental Psychology*, 1958, *55*, 543-553.

DOMHOFF, B. Home dreams versus laboratory dreams. In M. Kramer (Ed.) *Dream psychology and the new biology of dreaming*. Springfield, Ill.: Thomas, 1969.

DOMHOFF, B., & KAMIYA, J. Problems in dream content study with objective indicators — I: A comparison of home and laboratory dream reports. *Archives of General Psychiatry*, 1964, *11*, 519-524.

DREYFUS-BRISAC, C. The EEG of the premature infant and the full term newborn. In P. Kelloway & I. Peterson (Eds.), *Neurological and electroencephalogic correlative studies of infancy*. New York: Grune & Stratton, 1964.

EGGAN, D. The personal use of myth in dreams. *Journal of American Folklore*, 1955, *68*, 445-453.

EMPSOM, J., & CLARKE, P. Rapid eye movements and remembering. *Nature*, 1970, 287-288.

ERIKSON, E. The dream specimen in psychoanalysis. In R. Knight & C. Friedman (Eds.), *Psychoanalytic psychiatry and psychology*. New York: International Universities Press, 1954.

EVANS, C.R., & NEWMAN, E.A. Dreaming: An analogy from computers. *New Scientist*, 1964, *419*, 577-579.

FEINBERG, I. Eye movement activity during sleep and intellectual function in mental retardation. *Science*, 1968, *159*, 1256.

FEINBERG, I. Effects of age on human sleep patterns. In A. Kales (Ed.), *Sleep: Physiology and pathology.* Philadelphia: Lippincott, 1969.

FEINBERG, I., BRAUN, M., & SCHULMAN, E. EEG sleep patterns in mental retardation. *Electroencephalography and Clinical Neurophysiology,* 1969, *27,* 128.

FEINBERG, I., KORESKO, R., & GOTTLIEB, F. Further observations on electrophysiological sleep patterns in schizophrenia. *Comprehensive Psychiatry,* 1965, *6,* 21.

FEINBERG, I., KORESKO, R., GOTTLIEB, F., & WENDER, P. Sleep encephalographic and eye movement patterns in schizophrenic patients. *Comprehensive Psychiatry,* 1964, *5,* 44-53.

FEINBERG, I., KORESKO, R., & HELLER, N. EEG sleep patterns as a function of normal and pathological aging in man. *Journal of Psychiatric Research,* 1967, *5,* 107.

FISHBEIN, W., KASTANIOTIS, C., & CHATTMAN, D. Paradoxical sleep: Prolonged augmentation following learning. *Brain Research,* 1974, *79,* 61-75.

FISHER, C. Psychoanalytic implications of recent research on sleep and dreams. *Journal of the American Psychoanalytic Association,* 1965, *13,* 197-303.

FISHER, C., GROSS, J., & BYRNE, J. *Dissociation of penile erections from REMP and rebound effect.* Paper presented to the Association for the Psychophysiological Study of Sleep, Gainesville, Fla., 1965.

FISS, H., KLEIN, G., & BOKERT, E. Waking fantasies following interruptions of two types of sleep. *Archives of General Psychiatry,* 1965, *12,* 29-45.

FOULKES, D. Dream reports from different stages of sleep. *Journal of Abnormal and Social Psychology.* 1962, *65,* 14-25.

FOULKES, D. Non-rapid eye movement mentation. *Experimental Neurology,* 1967, Supplement 4, 28-38.

FOULKES, D., & RECHTSCHAFFEN, A. Presleep determinants of dream content: Effects of two films. *Perceptual and Motor Skills,* 1964, *19,* 983-1005.

FREUD, S. *The interpretation of dreams.* New York: Basic Books, 1955.

FROMM, E. *The forgotten language.* New York: Rinehart, 1951.

GARFIELD, P. *Creative dreaming.* New York: Simon & Schuster, 1974.

GIBSON, J. *The senses considered as perceptual systems.* Boston: Houghton Mifflin, 1966.

GILLIN, J., JACOBS, L., FRAM, D., WILLIAMS, R., & SNYDER, F. Partial REM deprivation in unmedicated psychiatric patients. *Psychophysiology,* 1972, *9,* 139.

GOODENOUGH, D., LEWIS, H., SHAPIRO, A., & SLESER, I. Some correlates of dream reporting following laboratory awakenings. *Journal of Nervous and Mental Disease,* 1965, *140,* 365-373.

GOTTSCHALK, L., & GLESER, G. *The measurement of psychological states through the content analysis of verbal behavior.* Berkeley: University of California Press, 1969.

GREENBERG, R., & DEWAN, E. Aphasia and rapid eye movement sleep. *Nature*, 1969, *223*, 183.

GREENBERG, R., KELTY, M., & DEWAN, E. *Sleep patterns in the newly hatched chick.* Paper presented to the Association for the Psychophysiological Study of Sleep, Boston, 1969.

GREENBERG, R., & PEARLMAN, C. Delirium tremens and dreaming. *American Journal of Psychiatry*, 1967, *124*, 133–142.

GREENBERG, R., PILLARD, R., & PEARLMAN, C. The effect of dream (stage REM) deprivation on adaptation to stress. *Psychosomatic Medicine*, 1972, *34*, 257–262.

GREENLEAF, E. Senoi dream groups. *Psychotherapy: Theory, Research, and Practice*, 1973, *10*, 218–222.

GRIESER, C., GREENBERG, R., & HARRISON, R. The adaptive function of sleep. *Journal of Abnormal Psychology*, 1972, *80*, 280–286.

GROSS, M., GOODENOUGH, D., TOBIN, M., HALPERT, E., LEPORE, D., PEARLSTEIN, A., SIROTA, M., DiBIANCO, J., FULLER, R., & KISHNER, I. Sleep disturbance and hallucinations in the acute alcoholic psychosis. *Journal of Nervous and Mental Disease*, 1966, *142*, 493–514.

GULEVITCH, G., DEMENT, E., & ZARCONE, V. All night sleep recordings of chronic schizophrenics in remission. *Comprehensive Psychiatry*, 1967, *8*, 141–149.

HALL, C. A cognitive theory of dreams. In S. Lee & A. Mayes (Eds.), *Dreams and dreaming.* Middlesex, England: Penguin, 1973.

HALL, C., & VAN DE CASTLE, R. Studies of dreams reported in the laboratory and at home. *Monograph Studies No. 1*, Institute of Dream Research, Santa Cruz, Cal., 1966.

HARTMANN, E. Dreaming sleep and the menstrual cycle. *Journal of Nervous and Mental Disease*, 1966, *143*, 406–416.

HARTMANN, E., BAEKELAND, F., & ZWILLING, G. Psychological differences between long and short sleepers. *Archives of General Psychiatry*, 1972, *26*, 463–468.

HAURI, P. The effects of evening activity on early night sleep. *Psychophysiology*, 1966, *4*, 267–277.

HAURI, P. White noise and dream reporting. *Sleep Research*, 1972, *1*, 122.

HOBSON, J.A., GOLDFRANK, F., & SNYDER, F. Respiration and mental activity in sleep. *Journal of Psychiatric Research*, 1965, *3*, 79–90.

ITIL, T. Changes in digital computer analyzed EEG during "dreams" and experimentally induced hallucinations. In W. Keup (Ed.), *Origin and mechanisms of hallucinations.* New York: Plenum Press, 1970.

Jackson, J.H. *Selected writings of John Hughlings Jackson.* Edited by J. Taylor. New York: Basic Books, 1958.

JENKINS, J., & DALLENBACH, K. Obliviscence during sleep and waking. *American Journal of Psychology*, 1924, *35*, 605–612.

JUNG, C. *Man and his symbols.* Garden City, N.Y.: Doubleday, 1964.

JUNG, C. *Analytical psychology: Its theory and practice.* New York: Pantheon, 1968.

KALES, A., HOEDEMAKER, F., JACOBSON, A., & LICHTENSTEIN, E. Dream deprivation: An experimental reappraisal. *Nature,* 1964, *204,* 1337-1338.

KLIENSMITH, L., & KAPLAN, S. Paired associate learning as a function of arousal and interpolated interval. *Journal of Experimental Psychology,* 1963, *65,* 190.

KLING, A., BOROWITZ, G., & CARTWRIGHT, R. Plasma levels of 17-hydroxycorticosteroids during sexual arousal in man. *Journal of Psychosomatic Research,* 1972, *16,* 215-221.

KORESKO, R., SNYDER, F., & FEINBERG, I. Dream time in hallucinating and nonhallucinating schizophrenic patients. *Nature,* 1963, *199,* 1118.

KRAMER, M., WHITMAN, R., BALDRIDGE, B., & LANSKY, L. Patterns of dreaming: The interrelationship of dreams of a night. *Journal of Nervous and Mental Disease,* 1964, *139,* 426.

KRAMER, M., WHITMAN, R., BALDRIDGE, B., & ORNSTEIN, P. Dream content in male schizophrenic patients. *Diseases of the Nervous System,* 1970, *31,* 51-58.

KRIPPNER, S., ULLMAN M., & VAUGHN, A. *Dream telepathy.* New York: Macmillan, 1973.

KUPFER, D., WYATT, R., SCOTT, J., & SNYDER, F. Sleep disturbance in acute schizophrenic patients. *American Journal of Psychiatry,* 1970, *126,* 1213-1223.

LAIRY, G., BARROS-FERREIRA, M., & GOLDSTEINAS, L. Les phases intermediaires du sommeil. In H. Gastaut, E. Lugaresi, G. Berti Ceroni, & C. Coccagna (Eds.), *The abnormalities of sleep in man.* Bologna: Aulo Gaggi, 1968.

LEWIS, H., GOODENOUGH, D., SHAPIRO, A., & SLESER, I. Individual differences in dream recall. *Journal of Abnormal Psychology,* 1966, *71,* 52-59.

MCNAIR, D., LORR, M., & DROPPLEMAN, L. *Profile of mood states.* San Diego, Calif.: Educational and Industrial Testing Service, 1971.

MEDNICK, S., & MEDNICK, M. *Remote Associates Test.* Boston: Houghton Mifflin, 1967.

MEIER, C. A Jungian view. In M. Kramer (Ed.), *Dream psychology and the new biology of dreaming.* Springfield, Ill.: Thomas, 1969.

MEIER, C., RUEF, H., ZIEGLER, A., & HALL, C. Forgetting dreams in the laboratory. *Perceptual and Motor Skills,* 1968, *26,* 551-557.

MURRAY, H. *Thematic Apperception Test.* Cambridge: Harvard University Press, 1938.

MUZIO, J., ROFFWARG, H., ANDERS, T., & MUZIO, L. Retention of rote-learned meaningful verbal material and alterations in normal sleep EEG patterns. *Psychophysiology,* 1972, *9,* 108.

NEISSER, U. *Cognitive psychology.* New York: Appleton-Century-Crofts, 1967.

OKUMA, T., SUNAMI, Y., FUKUMA, E., TAKEO, S., & MOTOIKE, M. Dream content study in chronic schizophrenics and normals by REMP-awakening technique. *Folia Psychiatrica et Neurologica Japonica*, 1970, *3*, 151-162.

OSWALD, I. Sleep and dependence on amphetamine and other drugs. In A. Kales (Ed.), *Sleep: Physiology and pathology*. Philadelphia: Lippincott, 1969.

PARMALEE, A. Maturation of EEG activity during sleep in premature infants. *Electroencephalography and Clinical Neurophysiology*, 1968, *24*, 319.

PIAGET, J. *The origins of intelligence in children*. New York: Norton, 1963.

PLATO. *The Republic*. Translated by F. McDonald. New York: Oxford University Press, 1945.

RECHTSCHAFFEN, A., VOGEL, G., & SHAIKUN, G. Interrelatedness of mental activity during sleep. *Archives of General Psychiatry*, 1963, *9*, 536-547.

ROFFWARG, H., MUZIO, J., & DEMENT, W. Ontogenetic development of the human sleep-dream cycle. *Science*, 1966, *152*, 604-619.

ROGERS,C. A theory of therapy, personality, and interpersonal relationships. In S. Koch (ed.), *Psychology: A study of a science* (Vol. 3). New York: McGraw-Hill, 1959.

SALAMY, J. Instrumental responding to internal cues associated with REM sleep. *Psychonomic Science*, 1970, *18*, 342-343.

SAMPSON, H. Deprivation of dreaming sleep by two methods. *Archives of General Psychiatry*, 1965, *13*, 79-86.

SCHONBAR, R. Differential dream recall frequency as a component of "life style." *Journal of Consulting Psychology*, 1965, *29*, 468-474.

SHAPIRO, A. Dreaming and the physiology of sleep: A critical review of some empirical data and a proposal for a theoretical model of sleep and dreaming. *Experimental Neurology*, 1967, Supplement 4, 56-81.

SHULMAN, B. An Adlerian view. In M. Kramer (Ed.), *Dream psychology and the new biology of dreaming*. Springfield, Ill.: Thomas, 1969.

SMITH, C., KITAHAMA, K., VALATX, J., & JOUVET, M. Increased paradoxical sleep in mice during acquisition of a shock avoidance task. *Brain Research*, 1974, *77*, 221-230.

SNYDER, F. *Dream recall, respiratory variability, and depth of sleep*. Paper presented to the American Psychiatric Association, Atlantic City, N.J., 1960.

SPIELBERGER, C., GORSUCH, R., & LUSHENE, R. *The State-Trait Anxiety Inventory*, Palo Alto, Calif.: Consulting Psychologists Press, 1969.

SPERRY, R.W. Hemisphere deconnection and unity in conscious awareness. *American Psychologist*, 1968, *23*, 723-733.

STARKER, S. Effects of sleep state and method of awakening upon Thematic Apperception Test productions at arousal. *Journal of Nervous and Mental Disease*, 1970, *150*, 188-194.

STEVENSON,R.L. A chapter on dreams. *Memories and portraits, random memories, memories of himself*. New York: Scribner's, 1925.

STEWART, K. Dream theory in Malaya. *Complex*, 1951, *6*, 21-34.

TART, C. Frequency of dream recall and some personality measures. *Journal of Consulting Psychology*, 1962, *26*, 467-470.

TAUBER, E., ROFFWARG, H., & HERMAN, J. The effects of long-standing perceptual alteration on the hallucinatory content of dreams. *Psychophysiology*, 1968, *5*, 219.

TRINDER, J., & KRAMER, M. Dream recall. *American Journal of Psychiatry*, 1971, *128*, 296-301.

VAN DE CASTLE, R.L. The psychology of dreaming. In S. Lee & A. Mayes (Eds.), *Dreams and dreaming*. Middlesex, England: Penguin, 1973.

VAN ORMER, E. Retention after intervals of sleep and waking. *Archives of Psychology*, 1932, *21*, 137.

VERDONE, P. Temporal reference of manifest dream content. *Perceptual Motor Skills*, 1965, *20*, 1253.

VOGEL, G. A review of REM deprivation. *Archives of General Psychiatry*, 1975, *32*, 749-761.

VOGEL, G., GIESLER, D., & BARROWCLOUGH, B. Exercise as a substitute for REM sleep. *Psychophysiology*, 1970, 7, 300-301.

VOGEL, G., THURMOND, A., GIBBONS, D., SLOAN, K., BOYD, M., & WALKER, M. Sleep reduction effects on depressive syndromes. *Archives of General Psychiatry*, 1975, *32*, 765-777.

VOGEL, G., & TRAUB, A. REM deprivation—I: The effect on schizophrenic patients. *Archives of General Psychiatry, 1968, 18*, 287.

WEBB, W., & AGNEW, H. Sleep: The effects of a restricted regime. *Science*, 1965, *150*, 1745-1747.

WEBB, W., & AGNEW, H. Sleep characteristics of long and short sleepers. *Science*, 1970, *168*, 146-147.

WEISZ, R., & FOULKES, D. Home and laboratory dreams collected under uniform sampling conditions. *Psychophysiology*, 1970, *6*, 588-597.

WITKIN, H., & LEWIS, H. Presleep experiences and dreams. In H. Witkin & H. Lewis (Eds.), *Experimental studies of dreaming*. New York: Random House, 1967.

ZARCONE, V., GULEVITCH, G., PIVIK, T., & DEMENT, W. Partial REM phase deprivation and schizophrenia. *Archives of General Psychiatry*, 1968, *18*, 194-202.

ZIMMERMAN, J., STOYVA, J., & METCALF, D. Distorted visual feedback and augmented REM sleep. *Psychophysiology*, 1970, *7*, 298.

ZIMMERMAN, W. Sleep mentation and auditory awakening thresholds. *Psychophysiology*, 1970, *6*, 540-549.

# INDEX